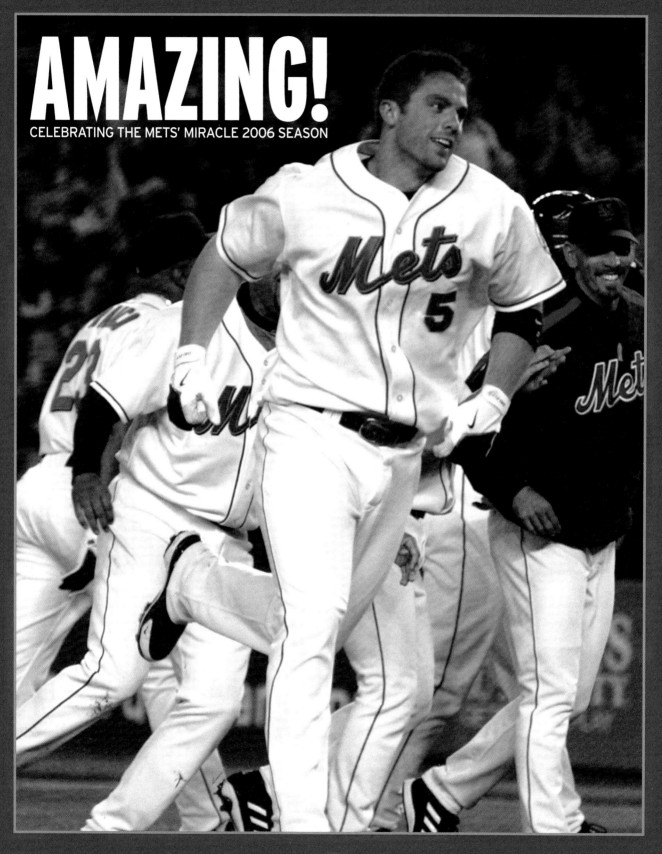

AMAZING!

CELEBRATING THE METS' MIRACLE 2006 SEASON

TRIUMPH
B O O K S

Published by Triumph Books, Chicago.

TEXT BY
KEVIN KERNAN

PHOTOGRAPHY BY
AP/WIDE WORLD PHOTOS

Content packaged by Mojo Media, Inc.
Editor: Joe Funk
Creative Director: Jason Hinman

This book is available in quantity at special discounts for your group or organization.
For further information, contact:

Triumph Books
542 South Dearborn Street
Suite 750
Chicago, IL 60605

Chicago, Illinois 60605
Phone: (312) 939-3330
Fax: (312) 663-3557

Printed in the United States of America

Contents

Meet Minaya's Mets
Aggressive GM Makes All The Right Moves

For Omar Minaya, it's always been about the magic of baseball, his passion for the game, the magic of Opening Day. He is so comfortable on the diamond, and he's at his best during batting practice, moving from player to player, speaking English or Spanish to get the pulse of his team.

About an hour before the Mets opened their 2006 season at Shea Stadium with a 3-2 win over the Washington Nationals, Minaya just completed such a round with players and coaches and sat on the bench in the Mets dugout. He talked about what Opening Day meant to a 9-year-old kid from Queens in 1969, an energetic kid who was always outside playing stickball. He talked about the magic the Mets made that year, when he would rush home to listen to the games on the radio. "We didn't have good TV reception," Minaya said.

What did he remember most about that day 37 years ago? What did he remember most about the 1969 Miracle Mets?

"The song," Minaya said with a smile. He then leaned back and broke into a decent American Idol version of "Meet the Mets, Greet the Mets ... "

"When you heard that song," he said, "it felt like spring."

For Minaya, the game means so many different things. Born in the Dominican, where the game is loved, Minaya became the first Hispanic general manager in the majors when he took over the Expos February 12, 2002. When he became Mets GM on

September 30, 2004, he landed his dream job. A fate of a franchise, his home franchise, rested on his shoulders. His goal was to improve the pitching and make the Mets more athletic.

After Minaya started making sweeping moves, some criticized him for adding too many Latin players to the Mets mix, a ridiculous assertion.

"I just don't even think about that," Minaya explained to columnist Dave Buscema of the Times Herald-Record in spring training. "I don't think about size, weight, religion. I think about talent. I'm a talent evaluator. And to me it's about a person's ability to play this game. I was fortunate enough to grow up in a neighborhood where we didn't even think about what others were. We were all New Yorkers. We all got along. I had a chance to grow up with people who came from all parts of the world. Learned different cultures, different ways."

Minaya's 2006 Mets got their first "W" on Opening Day, a season of promise was off to a great start, and his new rightfielder Xavier Nady picked up four hits, scored a run and drove in another. "One day is one day," cautioned Minaya, "but it's always nice to win."

As it turned out there would be much more winning for the Mets and a great part of that success can be directly tied to Minaya's bold decisions as executive vice president and general manager. The first key move in his reign came on December 16, 2004. That's when the Mets' new GM convinced Pedro

Omar Minaya and Willie Randolph discuss strategy during spring training in Port St. Lucie, Florida.

Jose Reyes and Omar Minaya share a laugh in Minaya's golf cart during spring training.

Martinez to sign as a free agent. That was a turning point for the downtrodden franchise.

No longer would Minaya, a former minor league outfielder, be looked upon as someone who was just a caretaker for the Expos, Major League Baseball's orphaned team. He became his own man with that stunning signing, stealing Martinez away from the World Champion Red Sox.

With that signature move, Minaya burst onto the big-market scene. George Steinbrenner and the Yankees took notice. Minaya did not want the Mets to be second-class citizens any longer. With the sign-ing of Pedro, New York was no longer just a Yankees town. The Mets were going to be serious Playerz. They would spend the money. They would get the big names. They would build the farm system it would take to keep the talent flowing through the majors.

They would become a proud, classy franchise.

Less than a month later, Minaya once again shocked the baseball world by signing free agent Carlos Beltran. Minaya had smashed two long home runs with his first two swings of the offseason and was just warming up. There was the opportunity to hit the longest of home runs, the chance to sign free agent Carlos Delgado.

Minaya and his staff knew that to make Beltran

Owner Jeff Wilpon and Omar Minaya pose for photos with their first-round draft choice, righthanded pitcher Mike Pelfry. The Mets and Pelfry finalized a $5.25 million, four-year contract after the pitcher passed a physical.

Gary Carter, Darryl Strawberry, Tim Teufel, Randy Niemann, and Howard Johnson, of the 1986 World Champion New York Mets, throw out the ceremonial first pitch prior to a game with the St. Louis Cardinals during spring training.

the player he would need to become in New York, the Mets had to sign Delgado. For all his greatness, Beltran needed help in the lineup. Big Papi needs Manny. Carlos I needed Carlos II.

The Marlins, though, beat Minaya to the punch and signed the free agent to a four-year, $52 million deal the last week of January.

If Minaya learned one thing during his years in scouting, it was patience. So when opportunity knocked again after the 2005 season, Minaya opened the door. On Thanksgiving, Minaya completed a trade with the cash-starved Marlins, stealing away Delgado for first baseman Mike Jacobs, right-handed pitcher Yusmeiro Petit and minor league

infielder Grant Psomas. He had his second big bat.

"When you look at championship teams, they usually have a presence," Minaya said at the time. The Mets had a presence with Delgado anchoring their lineup.

The only weakness appeared to be second base, where Kaz Matsui was returning. Quietly, Minaya had taken care of that problem by signing 36-year-old free agent Jose Valentin on December 8, 2005. No one realized that, though, until Valentin began to play every day. His $912,500 contract was one of the best bargains in baseball.

The biggest need was to add a shut-the-door closer. The Yankees had Mariano Rivera. No one could be like Rivera, but Minaya could get a closer with the same song: "Enter Sandman", and tremendous ability.

Enter Billy Wagner.

Five days after signing Delgado, Minaya signed the dominating lefty to a four-year, $43 million deal.

Pitching coach Rick Peterson instructs Yusaku Iriki, of Japan, through interpreter Nozomu Matsumoto.

Omar Minaya talks on the phone as he sits with Rickey Henderson watching the Mets beat the Yankees 8-3 during interleague play.

Big moves and little moves. All trades are not blockbusters, but they can be significant like the deal that sent Jae Seo to the Dodgers for reliever Duaner Sanchez that Minaya pulled off on January 4, 2006.

As every Met fan knows, just check out the entertaining websites mets-blog.com or metsgeek.com, a team is only as strong as its bullpen. Seo never fit in with pitching coach Rick Peterson. Peterson was convinced that Seo would never be a top of the rotation starter, but Sanchez had the ability to set up for Wagner. Scouts loved this deal when it was made.

To understand the importance of the bullpen, just go back to 2005 and the disaster that was Braden Looper. Looper blew the first game of the season that year in Cincinnati. That would have been Pedro's first win as a Met. Instead it became the first loss. The team quickly fell to 0-5. The tone was set. The bullpen was a problem the entire year.

Minaya was not going to allow that to happen in 2006. So he sent Seo and left-handed pitcher Tim Hamulack to the Dodgers for the 26-year-old Sanchez and right-hander Steve Schmoll. Wagner had been signed five weeks earlier, but now the bullpen was complete with Sanchez, Aaron Heilman, and Wagner as its key pieces.

On the morning of the trade deadline, July 31, Sanchez was involved in a car accident while riding as a passenger in a cab in Miami. He suffered a dislocated shoulder, underwent surgery and was out for the year. It was a terrible blow to the Mets.

Minaya had been working on adding a top of the rotation starter to the team, a stunning deal that could have bought the Mets Houston's Roy Oswalt or San Francisco's Jason Schmidt. Instead, the GM

"It seemed like all roads kind of led to New York," Wagner said.

All the pieces of the puzzle were coming together. A team that was a laughing stock had been transformed, almost overnight in baseball terms. In the space of 11 months, the Mets and Minaya had completed an Extreme Makeover that was the envy of all other GMs.

There were still key parts to add, intriguing little baseball additions, but the foundation of Pedro, Carlos I, Carlos II, and Billy the Kid were in place. The Mets and Minaya were on their way to their own magical season.

"Meet the Mets. Greet the Mets ..."

"There are no geniuses in baseball," Minaya would say more than once during the season. "Some deals work, some don't. You just keep trying to make moves to improve the club."

Picher Dae-Sung Koo of Korea takes part in a drill during a spring training baseball workout.

**Outfielder Carlos Beltran, GM Omar Minaya
and shortstop Jose Reyes, far right, socialize with
Jon Litner, third from left, after Litner announced
the formation of SportsNet New York in the
midtown Manhattan studios of the new regional
sports network.**

had to switch gears to beef up the bullpen. Nothing
is promised in baseball.

The good ones stay focused on the action, one
inning, one pitch at a time. So instead of getting a
starter, Minaya used the trading chip he had, Nady,
and sent him to the Pirates for reliever Roberto
Hernandez, who had been the Mets setup man in
2005, and lefty Oliver Perez, a project worth pursu-
ing. That deal meant that young outfielder Lastings

Milledge could not be used to acquire a top of the
rotation starter. Instead, he would move up from the
minors to play right field for the Mets.

Losing Sanchez hurt in many ways. He was
durable. In 2005 he tied for second in the National
League in appearances and held right-handed batters to a .182 mark. His final 22 outings of the season opponents hit only .188 against him. Minaya's
reason for making the Sanchez deal was simple. "I
felt we had to make sure we got the ball to Billy
Wagner," he explained. "The seventh and eighth
innings are very crucial innings. Sanchez was a
good fit for us."

That's why he had to be replaced quickly. A team
with a 14-game lead in the National League East
suddenly was vulnerable in the seventh and eighth

Yusako Iriki takes a warm-up throw during an early spring game with the St. Louis Cardinals.

innings, and because Nady had to go, Milledge was thrust into the spotlight. Minaya said he had faith in Milledge, saying, "I feel this kid has the ability and the confidence to step in and do some things. A lot of things have prepared him for this."

Minaya could have been talking about himself. A lot of things prepared him for his dream job and he was going to make the most of it, no matter what obstacles came his way. Minaya had learned baseball is more than just assembling stars, there had to be role players, too. There had to be chemistry.

The trading of Mike Cameron to the Padres for Nady back on November 18, 2005, was critical. Cameron was never happy with having been moved to right field to make way for Beltran and felt he was the better center fielder of the two. The deal would give him the chance to play center every day and it would give the Mets the solid right fielder they needed. Part of being a GM is making a trade that is good for both teams. Everyone wins and there are more trading opportunities in the future. Baseball is a game of relationships and Minaya is well liked by the other GMs.

"We don't get Delgado unless we move Cameron," Minaya said of Cameron's $7.3 million salary. Minaya and his scouting crew, assistant GM Tony Bernazard and special assistant Sandy Johnson, were beginning to see a winning team take shape with that November trade.

Some trades are outright steals. The Paul Lo Duca trade was just such a deal. The Mets needed a defensive-minded catcher after letting Mike Piazza walk away as a free agent. The Marlins needed to save money and gave Lo Duca away for two minor leaguers, outfielder Dante Brinkley and right-handed pitcher Gaby Hernandez the first week of December, an early Christmas present. A few days later ageless Julio Franco was signed as a free agent. Adding Lo Duca and Franco brought the Mets together as a team. Part of being successful in New York is knowing when to use money as a chip. The Yankees have been doing it for years.

"Lo Duca knows how to lead a pitching staff," said former Marlins manager Jack McKeon. "He was just what the Mets needed. Omar made a great trade there."

Some trades are made for more than just on-the-field reasons. Minaya dealt Kris Benson the third week of January to Baltimore for John Maine, who would develop into a solid starter, and reliever Jorge Julio, because Benson's wife had become a distraction. When she openly criticized Delgado, Benson was soon traded.

It all comes back to scouting for Minaya. "I believe in my scouts," Minaya has said time and again. Why not? He began as a scout with the Texas Rangers in 1985 after playing outfield in the A's and Mariners organizations and spending time playing baseball in Italy in 1983-84.

Minaya started by scouting in his native Dominican and by 1990 was named the Rangers' director of professional and international scouting. Two years later he became the Mets' assistant GM. He left the Mets for the Expos in 2002.

After the Mets' disastrous 2004 season, and the terrible trade that sent Scott Kazmir to the Devil Rays for Victor Zambrano on July 30, owner Fred Wilpon turned to Minaya to save his team.

The 9-year-old kid from Queens could finally Meet his Mets.

Minaya's goal was to get his team to the postseason. "Get to the playoffs and see what happens," he explained. "Anything can happen."

You can be sure of this, no matter how much success the Mets have in 2006, Minaya will not sit back and rest on his laurels. "I don't allow myself time to rest," said the father of two boys. "I enjoy what I'm doing and I enjoy the challenge, but not resting. The only time I take a moment to rest is when I look at my kids. I think when you rest, you're dropping your guard." ●

Billy Wagner looks like an infielder during a spring training drill.

Mr. Motivation

Randolph's Winning Attitude Is Contagious

At first, Mets fans didn't quite understand Willie Randolph. Many of them looked at him as a Yankee product, not as a Met.

They couldn't have been more wrong. They didn't see that Randolph became manager of the Mets for one reason: He wanted to make them into a championship team. Randolph's best trait is that he is not afraid to put pressure on himself, and he's not afraid to demand excellence.

"I've never felt pressure as a player or a manager," Randolph said of his second year as manager of the Mets. "When you compete as much as I have over my career you kind of get used to that. You feel that's the way it is. It becomes second nature. I understand what pressure is and what it means, but I feel good in that environment.

"As long as I work hard, and teach and communicate and try to prepare my guys for the game then when the game starts it's like 'OK,' then if you have to tweak anything, you make sure you do that the next game," he said. "That's what's great about baseball, you got a long season and you continue to get better hopefully as you go."

That's what Randolph, 51, did during his 18-year major league career as a player. He was a natural leader from the first time he stepped onto a baseball field.

Mets fans are beginning to understand that Randolph will get the most out of all his players and will sometimes go about unorthodox means to get the job done. He will challenge them. He will push them. It's up to them to respond.

"These guys know I am going to come out at them hard, come at them strong," Randolph explained, "but they know that I'm trying to help. Hopefully they won't tell me to shut up."

"If he likes you," said his son Andre, 25, who played briefly in the Yankee organization, "he will joke with you. A lot of people don't realize he has a great sense of humor."

Randolph has shown himself to be quite the motivator. You can't spend all that time in the majors and all that time around Joe Torre as a coach and not learn what makes players tick.

In many ways, Randolph is a motivator as much as he is a manager. The two go hand in hand. Consider this story from TV star Kelly Ripa.

Back in 2001, Ripa, who was friends with Willie and his lovely wife Gretchen, sat in Randolph's kitchen in Franklin Lakes, New Jersey, listening intently for 45 minutes to words of encouragement from Willie.

These would be the same types of words Willie would use to motivate the Mets when he took over the team four years later. "Xs and Os are one thing," Randolph said of his new job at the time, "but you need to motivate people and get them to trust you. To get these guys to run through a wall for you is really what managing is all about."

That day in 2001, Kelly Ripa listened intently. She was about to embark on a new job with Regis Philbin. She was about to become co-host of *Live! With Regis and Kelly*.

Willie Randolph congratulates Billy Wagner on his 300th save after the Mets' 7-6, come-from-behind victory over the Pittsburgh Pirates.

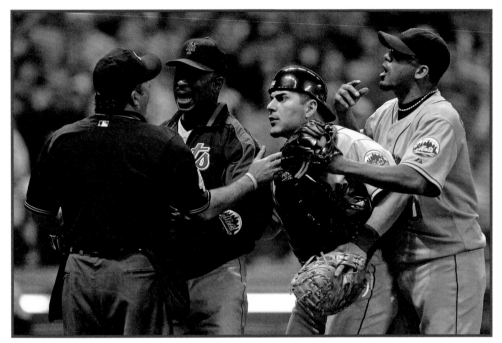

Willie Randolph, catcher Paul Lo Duca, and pitcher Duaner Sanchez argue with umpire Tim Tschida, left, during the ninth inning of a game against the Milwaukee Brewers.

That's when Randolph decided to put on his baseball face and for the next 45 minutes gave Ripa a pep talk. Randolph's hope and faith ruled the day.

"I knew Kelly would be a success," Willie would say later. "She's smart, competitive, beautiful, and funny as all get-out. I told her, 'You got to believe in yourself, kid, you can do this. Kathie Lee was there for a long time. She did great, but you can be better than her. Don't be intimidated by Regis. Work hard. You can deal with this guy.' "

Ripa is eternally grateful for the kind words.

"Willie gave me the pep talk of my life," Ripa said of that life-changing day. "He told me, 'You are the right person for this job, give 110 percent, do things the right way—that's the way you live your life and you will not fail. Be yourself.' This man is an amazing motivator. He noticed qualities about me that I didn't notice I had. He said, 'This is your job, this is your moment!'

"I was so pumped when I left there, my head wouldn't fit through the door." In fact, Ripa was so excited she told Randolph, "You know, you should be a motivational speaker or you should really coach a team or something."

Recalling the scene and living up to her zany image, Ripa added, "Willie smiled at me and said, 'Kelly, I coach third base for the New York Yankees.' That's right,' I said, 'I forgot.' "

No one is forgetting about Randolph now. Whenever the Mets have needed a jolt in 2006 he has been there to give them one. Randolph takes nothing for granted even after winning all those championships with the Yankees as a player and coach.

Willie and Gretchen became friends with actor Mark Consuelos of *All My Children* fame 12 years ago when they met at a charity function. "He's a big Yankee fan and Gretchen is a big soap-opera fan," Willie said. One day, Mark asked if he could bring a friend over for dinner. That friend turned out to be daytime diva Kelly Ripa, who played Hayley Vaughan on the soap opera.

Consuelos and Ripa eventually married and moved near the Randolphs because they loved the neighborhood. The friendship blossomed and so did the careers of the two actors.

So then Kelly was about to get her big break, becoming Regis' right-hand girl, replacing Kathie Lee Gifford, but she was having second thoughts. The job was too daunting.

She told Willie, "I can't do this. What if they don't like me?"

Former Kansas City Monarchs manager Buck O'Neil greets New York's Willie Randolph.

Willie Randolph and his players celebrate with Jose Valentin after his two-out, 10th-inning, game-winning RBI single to give the Mets a 1-0 victory over the Chicago Cubs.

It's all about work ethic, something he learned from his father, growing up in Brooklyn. "My dad was a construction worker, cement and jackhammer, that kind of stuff," Randolph explained. "My dad and I probably never had a catch together, but he taught me the meaning of hard work. I saw him every day getting up early, coming in late, covered from head to toe in dirt and cement. He'd get a bath, get something to eat, watch TV, go to sleep and do it all over again the next day."

If you bring that same approach to a baseball field, you really have an edge. Randolph pumps up all his players, everyone from Carlos Delgado to Endy Chavez.

Chavez blossomed this year under Randolph. "He's been tremendous, man," Randolph told reporters in July. "He's, to me, one of the best fourth or fifth outfielders, whatever you want to label him, in the game. Defensively, there's no one better. He can throw, does a little bit of everything. [He has] speed and he's got-

ten some big hits."

Then there was the game on July 26 where Randolph went to the mound instead of pitching coach Rick Peterson. He personally wanted to deliver a message to young pitcher John Maine.

"I just had this sense that this was a huge moment for this kid," Randolph said after the game. So Randolph challenged Maine to dig deeper, that it was his game, his moment. Don't let it slip by.

Similar to the words he told Kelly Ripa back in 2001. Her job, her moment.

It worked for Ripa. It worked for Maine. David Wright said one of the first times he talked to Randolph, the new manager got him all pumped up about playing for him. "The energy that Willie has just rubs off on the rest of the team and it's an exciting place to be," Wright explained.

Randolph wants his team to be like a family. He wants them to care for one another, guide one another and, if needed, discipline one another. He is big on the "R" word–responsibility, something that has been lost in the permissive society. But he also wants you to have fun while playing the game. In some ways, Randolph is a lot like another manager enjoying great success in 2006, Detroit's Jim Leyland. Both come from the school that you are responsible for your actions: Don't blame someone else. Look in the mirror first.

As you can tell, Randolph is big on baseball and family. With his first signing bonus in 1972, Willie brought his mother a color TV. "A console color TV," he recalled with a smile. His first year as a Yankee in 1976, Randolph made $19,000. He made seven All-Star teams during a career that spanned 18 seasons. He owns six championship rings, two as a player, four as a coach. He played in four World Series and more games at second base (1,688) than any other Yankee. That is one impressive resume. And he just didn't take

Willie Randolph bites his lip as he walks off the field after taking starting pitcher Steve Trachsel out of a rain-delayed game against the Cincinnati Reds.

any managing job that came along. He wanted to manage in New York and waited for the right time.

Omar Minaya gave Randolph his chance when he named Randolph the 18th manager in Mets history on November 4, 2004. The team had just completed three straight horrible seasons, one under Bobby Valentine and the last two under Art Howe. The Mets needed to get things right. Randolph compiled an 83-79 record his rookie year as manager. He became only the third rookie manager to finish with a winning record after inheriting a team that was at least 20 games below .500 the previous year.

The other two managers to make such a dramatic change were the Angels' Mike Scioscia in 2000 and the Mets' Davey Johnson in 1984. Randolph had begun to change the losing culture of the Mets.

Randolph's playing career ended in 1992 with the Mets. Always a student of the game, Randolph also is a student of black history. Becoming the first African-American manager in New York means much to him.

"Knowing what the players went through in the past, I feel like I'm now part of that legacy," Randolph said. "If it wasn't for those forefathers who played the game with passion and a love for the game, I wouldn't be here. More than anything, in my mind, I want to make those players proud of the job I do."

Legends like Jackie Robinson and Cool Papa Bell. One of the best things about Randolph's approach is that he just doesn't hand the keys to the kingdom to a young, talented player. He makes that player earn playing time. Randolph has a way of keeping the competition flowing through the clubhouse. That competition is a way of challenging players and makes them better. That's how he brought along both Jose Reyes and Wright.

Of Wright, Randolph said before the 2005 season, "He has a great makeup. He works hard. I love that in my young players. I'm looking forward to watching this kid step up to certain levels, because he's just a baby. Long way to go."

Wright and Reyes have developed wonderfully under Randolph's tutelage. Another aspect Mets players respect about Randolph is his desire to improve. In spring training before Randolph's second year of managing, veteran pitcher Tom Glavine noted that in Randolph's first year, "Willie did a good job handling players and handling the game, but there's no question it's all going to get better.

"He really has a desire to work at managing and get better at it," the lefty added. "He's not going to tell you that he was perfect and did everything right. There's definitely that aura about him as a player that he is striving to manage the game better. When you see a manager working that hard, as a player, how do you not work hard?" Glavine added.

Randolph has gotten the Mets to work hard and he is not afraid to take on big-time pressure, saying from the beginning the Mets had the talent to win the NL East. When bumps in the road developed, he quickly addressed them. When reliever Pedro Feliciano criticized Randolph's use of the bullpen in early July, the manager met with Feliciano and made it clear that he would not tolerate such talk, noting, "I've been around winners my whole life," he said. "That's not what they do."

Randolph owns 17 years of post-season experience as a player and coach. His message was delivered loud and clear.

Randolph is not the type of manager to allow a team to rest on its laurels. Even though the Mets built a huge lead at the All-Star break, Randolph went into the second half of the season with a purpose. Randolph is always focused on doing the best he can at that moment.

"We had a great first half," Randolph said after the All-Star break. "The real season starts now. We're here to play the game the right way and to sacrifice for each other."

Come October, you could be sure he would repeat those words again.

"The real season starts now."

The man knows how to motivate. ●

Willie Randolph congratulates pitcher John Maine after Maine pitched a complete game against the Houston Astros at Shea Stadium. Maine held the Astros scoreless on four hits in the Mets' 7-0 win.

Magic Moments: April

There's Something Special In The Air

Twenty years ago Straw, Doc, Nails, Mookie, Mex, the Kid and Davey led the Mets to their second and last World Championship. That team was beloved by New Yorkers for their character and the indisputable fact they were characters.

They never quit, and they did it their way, having loads of fun along the way. On the field they played the game right. They played for each other and they played for their loyal fans. For most of those players that championship season was the apex of their careers. Life would never be as innocent or successful as it was that magical summer of 1986.

These 2006 Mets have a sense of confidence about them much like the 1986 Mets. And these new Mets also have youthful energy and innocence mixed with veteran know-how and proven talent, a wonderful combination.

Pedro, Carlos I, Carlos II, David, Jose and Paulie had a similar approach as the Mets of 20 years ago. They knew they could get the job done and make their own magic.

From Day 1 the expectations were huge for the 2006 Mets. That's just the way Willie Randolph wanted it to be.

"I'm not going to try to hide anything, the reality is the expectations are there," the manager said. "I don't like to put extra pressure on them. I'm just being honest."

Willie welcomed the expectations and this is what he told his Mets when they first got together as a team. "We've got a chance for something real special here. We've got a good ballclub, man. You want to be able to play in the postseason. You want to be part of something special. Let's go. Let's do it."

Let's do it.

With those words the Mets roared into the 2006 season.

"I don't have to be in your face about it," Randolph said, "but the bottom line is they are going to feel my passion for winning, and my passion for what I feel this club can do."

Randolph and the Mets had the chance to show everyone just how good they would be in a National League that was filled with mediocrity. April was to be the start of something big.

"The reality is we have a chance to have a lot of fun this year," Randolph said. "I want these guys to feel that, believe that, and expect that. If you don't, then why are we here?"

***

The fun started on Opening Day with a 3-2 win over the Nationals at Shea Stadium that showed a little bit of everything these Mets were capable of doing.

Tom Glavine allowed only one run over six innings. He gave them the kind of outing they would need from their starters all season long. The lefty had reinvented himself and would win 11 games by June 23.

When the Mets needed to score a run that Opening Day, they found a way. Everything from a bloop sin-

David Wright hits a seventh-inning, two-run triple off Florida Marlins pitcher Dontrelle Willis in the Mets' 3-2 win over the Marlins. Wright was responsible for all three runs the Mets scored.

New York Mets relief pitcher Jorge Julio leaves the field after being taken out of the game by Willie Randolph in the tenth inning against the Washington Nationals.

gle by new catcher Paul Lo Duca to young third baseman David Wright's impressive opposite-field home run. The Mets played terrific defense all day, including centerfielder Carlos Beltran throwing out Jose Vidro at second for the final out of the game.

That was a signal that a new day had dawned for Beltran, who was hampered by the expectations his first year as a Met and by injuries.

When that first game of the season ended, there was one huge difference from 2005. The Mets had

Billy Wagner on the mound, which changed the way opponents felt about the Mets. The bullpen was no longer without a legitimate shut-the-door closer. Wagner showed his class by saying, "That's how you get 280-something saves, guys picking you up and making plays."

On this day Wagner admitted he was as nervous as a high school kid making his first varsity start. He was not at his best but he got the job done and put it all into perspective, saying: "You got to have a little magic when you play."

His entrance music is the same as Mariano Rivera's with 'Enter Sandman' and Mets fans heard it for the first time. They loved it. Some Yankee fans were upset by it.

Billy Wagner pumps his fist after a particularly sweet win against the Atlanta Braves. Wagner earned a save, giving Pedro Martinez his 200th career win as the Mets defeated the Braves 4-3.

Xavier Nady scores a run during the fourth inning as Washington Nationals catcher Brian Schneider attempts to make the tag.

During the off-season Wagner was asked if he had ever been to Broadway. "I walked by it," he said. "I've never had time, I come to New York, I have to work."

Wagner, despite some setbacks, was prepared for New York. "Everybody knows New York is tough," he said. "But they haven't had to go out on the mound, either. I'm more suited for New York now than I was two or three years ago."

So was Randolph.

After a year on the job, Randolph showed what kind of team he would make the Mets into, a team that could win in many different ways, not just a Yankee way. "I never came in with any Yankees way," Randolph said. "I've been with different teams over my career, I didn't come here trying to be like the Yankees system or things like that."

A winning system needed to be developed and April was the perfect time to implement the plan. "We still have a lot to learn about winning and about each other," Randolph said. "It's not just about numbers, it's about your mental approach to the game and how you feel about the ultimate goal, and that's winning, how do you get to that next level. I'm not going to predict anything, but I feel great about what this team can do."

Then he offered what is the essence of his baseball beliefs: "The translation for winning," Randolph noted, "is everyone playing for each other."

Like the 1986 Mets did. Like the 1969 Miracle Mets did.

There would be no shortcuts, the Mets would have to come together as a team to get the job done. They would have to believe in themselves and make

Jose Reyes slides into second beneath leaping Milwaukee Brewers second baseman Bill Hall on Paul Lo Duca's at-bat in the bottom of the fifth inning of the Mets' 9-3 win over Milwaukee.

the world believe in them.

In that opener on a raw April day, Lo Duca pulled off just such a belief play when in the eighth inning, he tagged out Alfonso Soriano at home when he bobbled the ball without any of the rotating umpires noticing it. Most of the crowd of 54,371, the largest Opening Day crowd in Shea history, saw what happened, the Mets got away with something on that play. "You just show it and sell it," Lo Duca explained. Tim Tschida came down from first to cover the play. "I had the umpire screened," Lo Duca said.

But they also made something happen. Newly acquired Xavier Nady went 4-for-4, knocked in a run and scored one, too. Wright had his homer and Lo Duca had his RBI bloop hit. Beltran, who went 0-for-4, had to put up with the boos. "The important thing is we won," he explained. At that point, Beltran was saying the right words but if you looked into his eyes, you could tell he was hurt with the booing picking up where it left off last season. By throwing out Vidro at second, Beltran had put the fans on notice that the game is played on the field as well as in the batter's box.

Across the clubhouse, Cliff Floyd was upset by the crowd reaction to Beltran, saying, "That's not right. The thing is when you boo my teammate, you are booing me, too. I take it personally, we all do in here."

Wright agreed with Floyd, saying, "This isn't right." Wright, a fan favorite, could not grasp what the fans were doing to Beltran because those same fans already were starting with the MVP chants for him.

With one game, and one victory, the Mets were already far ahead of where they were last year when they didn't put up their first "W" until Game 6 of the season. Opening Day usually is a good day for the Mets. Over their history they are 28-17 on Opening Day.

"This was pretty special," said Glavine, who won his 276th game. "Today you got a glimpse of what they were expecting from all the guys we brought in here."

Noted Nady: "This is a neat way to start."

***

One week does not make a season, but David Wright was off to a blistering start and his two-run triple off Dontrelle Willis, one of the best pitchers in the game, in the seventh innning of a game in the following series tied the score at 2-2, and then he lifted the game-winning sacrifice fly in the ninth as the Mets pulled out a 3-2 victory over the Marlins on April 9. The win put the Mets at 4-2.

Wright worked hard in the off-season and throughout spring training at hitting the ball the other way and these were two more pay-off at-bats for him. At 23, he was already showing signs that he is the Mets' said Derek Jeter, hitting .479 with two home runs and nine RBI after one week.

Paul Lo Duca put Wright's start in perspective, "The kid's a special player. He's one of those types who has a knack to get a hit when you need it. You can't teach that. He's a young superstar, bottom line."

You can teach players to go to the opposite field, if they are willing to learn. Jeter has made a living on it and Wright is trying to do the same. "If you look at the great hitters in the game," the young third baseman said, "they go the other way just as well as they pull the ball. And I think that's something I'm learning."

The Mets were off to their best start since 1985.

***

West Coast trips are never easy for East Coast teams. There is the long flight, the change in time zone and early in the year it is especially difficult because after so many weeks in spring training, your body is not quite ready for such a jolt.

When you are 47 years old, however, evidently none of that matters. Just look at what Julio Franco did in the Mets resounding 7-2 win over the Padres on April 20, a win that showed just how tough the Mets were going to be on the road this season. That victory

Ramon Castro is safe at second as the Atlanta Braves' Tony Pena can't grab the throw during the sixth inning of an April game.

A giant New York Mets baseball cap is placed on the roof of a building in Midtown Manhattan during a promotional event in New York.

moved them to 4-0 away from Shea.

Then again, going to beautiful San Diego, self-proclaimed as America's Finest City, is usually a pick-me-up for tourists, and Franco was no different.

From the gorgeous homes in the hills of La Jolla to the beach bum feel of Pacific Beach, the city has a way to make you relax. Petco Park is located downtown and is a work of art. Take a break from the game and you can walk out to one of the outdoor bars and watch the sailboats cruise under the Coronado Bridge or just enjoy a margarita and a fish taco as the sun sets.

Franco showed that the sun is not setting on his career even though, incredibly so, he had already

David Wright watches his ninth-inning sacrifice fly that allowed Carlos Beltran to score the winning run in the Mets' 3-2 win over the Florida Marlins.

been in pro ball nine seasons and had been in the majors for four years the last time the Mets won the World Series in 1986.

When the Mets exploded for a six-run eighth inning, Franco got the action going with a two-run, opposite-field home run off reliever Scott Linebrink.

That home run made Franco the oldest player in Major League history to homer. When Franco crossed home plate he was 47 years, 240 days old. The record had been held by the Philadelphia Athletics' Jack Quinn, who was a relative baby compared to Franco. When he homered back in 1930 he was 46 years 357 days old. And no, Franco had not yet been born.

Franco was thinking team first after the home run, telling reporters, "It means a lot because we won the ballgame, first of all." Franco wanted to make sure people know he is a Met because of his ability, not his age. That's not clearly understood. "They don't see my ability," he said. "They see my age."

While Franco came up big, Carlos Beltran came up lame. Petco Park has not been good to him. He was shelved because of a sore right hamstring. This also was the first meeting the Mets had with their Hall of Fame catcher Mike Piazza, who signed with the Padres as a free agent. "It's been great," Piazza said of being in San Diego. "I mean, just look around."

The night also featured an inside-the-park home run by Kaz Matsui, who just joined the Mets from a rehab assignment. The homer was basically his last hurrah as a Met. It marked, incredibly, the third straight season that Matsui's first at-bat resulted in a home run.

This was only the third week of April but Amazin' stuff was already happening.

***

All classics aren't played in October, some are played in April. The Mets and Giants hooked up for just such a game in San Francisco on April 26, a three hour, 50-minute, 11-inning affair, that the Mets won, 9-7.

The game was sent into extra innings when pinch-hitter Barry Bonds turned around a Billy Wagner 99-mph fastball with two outs in the ninth inning. He only got a chance to hit because David Wright made an error. Wagner went right after Bonds. "My strength is his strength," Wagner said.

Wagner has a deep appreciation of Bonds because when Wagner was a young pitcher with the Astros going through a difficult period, Bonds spent nearly an hour with him before a game, giving him a pep talk. "That's something I will never forget," Wagner said.

On the home run, Wagner put the pitch right where he wanted it but Bonds took it to left-center for the home run. Asked by reporters if anyone else could have hit that pitch out, Wagner answered, "Maybe the Babe." Bonds said he never hit a ball like that off Wagner.

The home run was No. 711 for Bonds, which put him three away from tying Babe Ruth. The Mets won the game in the 11th when Chris Woodward smacked a tie-breaking double, but lost rookie pitcher Brian Bannister earlier in the game to a hamstring injury.

The tide was finally turning. The Mets were determined to put an end to the Braves' run of 14 straight division titles. At the end of the month they had the opportunity to make a statement game and they did just that on April 29, beating the Braves, 1-0 behind ex-Brave Tom Glavine. The lone run came on Paul Lo Duca's home run. The night before Pedro Martinez beat the Braves. The Mets' 1-2 Hall of Fame punch scored an early knockout.

The win secured the Mets' first series win at Turner Field in three years and increased their lead to seven games.

The win was their fourth in a row and the sixth in nine games of the road trip that also had stops in San Diego and San Francisco.

"It's still April," David Wright cautioned, "But it's definitely a step in the right direction."

Definitely. ●

Billy Wagner delivers a pitch in the ninth inning of the Mets' 3-2 win over the Florida Marlins. Wagner was the winning pitcher in the game.

All The Wright Moves

The Mets' Young Superstar Is Making It Big And Keeping It Real

David Wright knows how to make the most of New York. The third baseman with the million-dollar smile is the darling of the Mets fans at 23. He's been on *Letterman*. He hit a home run in his first All-Star Game. The night before that he exploded onto the national scene, pounding 16 home runs in the first round of the Home Run Derby.

He's got a great apartment in Manhattan and may be the most eligible bachelor in baseball, averaging about 12 marriage proposals a week. And he's got a big, fat contract that is guaranteed to pay him $55 million over the next six years.

Not bad for someone who was sleeping in a bunk bed at his family's home in Virginia just a few winters ago. Not bad for someone who had to have Mets public relations guru Jay Horwitz sneak him into the National League clubhouse in Houston at the 2004 All-Star Game, just so Wright could meet his idol, Scott Rolen.

When David Letterman showed a series of pictures with Wright's tongue hanging out, Wright said, "I figured Michael Jordan had a pretty good career and he stuck his tongue out, so I try to copy him."

Be like Mike. Why not? The best thing about Wright is that he has not forgotten where he comes from. With a dog named Homer and three younger brothers who keep him in line, how could he get a big head? "My three brothers won't allow that to happen," Wright promised.

It won't be long before Wright wins an MVP award, but don't expect him to change. That boyish smile will be on his face for a long, long time. His is a Wonderful Life and when he's home in Chesapeake, Va. or when his brothers come to visit in New York or travel to the All-Star Game with him in Pittsburgh, David plays the role of Big Brother to the max. He beats on them and they beat on him.

At home in Virginia during the winter, he drops them off at basketball practice or takes them out with him to go bowling--even on Christmas night, and yes, his date did come along. What was Wright's prized Christmas gift? An electronic dartboard.

It's all about competition with the Wright Brothers. "They even compete when they eat," explained his father Rhon, a captain in the Norfolk Police Department.

All Wright's hits aren't on the diamond. When he recently gave a tour of his family home, David crossed paths with younger brother Matt in an upstairs hallway. He instinctively gave Matt a punch to the chest. Matt merely "dusted off" the brother-blow with his right hand as the tour continued.

Anyone who has a brother or is the parent of boys could immediately relate. Matt, by the way, had gotten David good in a recent paint-ball battle. "It wasn't good enough to shoot me," David explained at the time. "He had to go and shoot my cell phone."

Boys will be boys. "You should see the welts they come home with," said his mom, Elisa.

Willie Randolph congratuates David Wright after the Mets' 9-4 win over the Baltimore Orioles. Wright hit a grand slam and drove in five runs in the win.

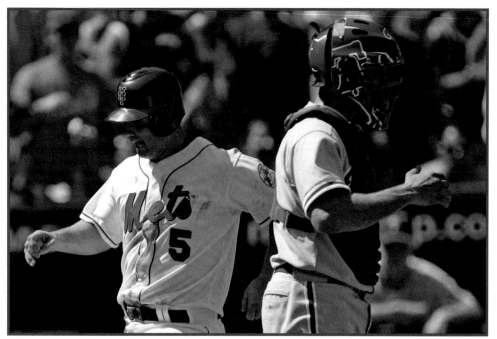

David Wright crosses home plate behind Philadelphia Phillies catcher Chris Coste to score on a double by Endy Chavez during the sixth inning. The Mets defeated the Phillies 4-3.

Most of all, Wright is there for family, friends and teammates. His AAU baseball coach, Towney Townsend, has been battling throat cancer for years. Wright and fellow major league players from the area have stepped up to help Townsend, players like Minnesota's Michael Cuddyer, Tampa Bay's B.J. Upton and Washington's Ryan Zimmerman.

They ran a golf outing to raise money to help pay medical expenses. Wright and his pals also take charge of a hitting camp for local kids every Christmas.

Wright is squeaky clean, although Rhon did admit there was that one time at Hickory High when David got into big trouble: He threw a hamburger during a food fight. "The great thing about David," said Cuddyer, who is only four years older but is Wright's mentor, "is that he would never do anything to hurt his image. I don't care what anybody says, we are role models and David knows it's important to be a good role model."

Said Townsend of Wright's success at such a young age, "David has what I call the sixth tool, the ability to forget something bad instantly and move on. I'm telling you, when it's all said and done, David will be one of the greatest players to ever play the game."

That's high praise, but that's how Wright is on the path of success. In many ways, he may be the most mature player in the Mets clubhouse and his ability is off the charts. Wright can hit for average and power and will only get better.

Wright produced 20 home runs, 74 RBI and a .316 average the first half of the 2006 season, good enough to be in the Top 10 in the NL in each of those categories and lead the Mets into first place and be voted starting third baseman in the All-Star Game. Wright also positioned himself to be considered a legitimate MVP candidate.

"That kid is special," fellow All-Star Tom Glavine said. "He's certainly been what he's been built up to be and more than that. There are a lot of similarities between David and Scott Rolen, not only in how they play but in how they go about learning the game and how they handle themselves."

Above all else, Wright can roll with the punches. He is no pampered star.

Consider his trip to Pittsburgh from New York. The Mets arranged for their All-Stars to arrive in two private jets. Turns out the jet Wright was trav-

Third baseman David Wright backhands a ground ball during a game against the Phillies in Philadelphia.

Carlos Delgado celebrates the Mets' 4-3 win over the Yankees with closer Billy Wagner as third baseman David Wright joins in.

eling on had an oil leak.

"I get off the plane, another plane comes," Wright said. "We finally get here and my agents arrange for a limo to pick me up and take me to Heinz Field for a party. We're going to roll up in style, but the limo driver was like a cab driver from New York. He ran over a curb and all of a sudden we have a flat tire. The guy wants to keep going and we're banging along on three wheels."

At that point, Wright was still a long walk from the party.

"I had two choices," Wright said. "Walk to the party or us pulling up in a limo, riding on the rims."

He opted to walk.

Despite all that, Wright had the time of his life in his first All-Star appearance. "I was like a kid in a candy store, going around getting autographs," Wright said, noting the two autographs he wanted the most were David Ortiz and Manny Ramirez.

Manny Being Manny, was not at the All-Star Game.

"I had a blast in the Home Run Derby, my brothers were on the field, it was great," Wright said. "At the very least I exceeded the expectations in the Mets clubhouse. Cliff Floyd said I would only hit two home runs. The whole experience, the derby, the game, was unbelievable. As a kid you dream about something like this."

Then in his first All-Star at-bat, he homered. "I just decided I was going to swing hard at the first pitch," he said.

Wright is a clutch player. Heading into the final stage of the 2006 season he was batting .381 with runners in scoring position and .311 from the seventh inning on, showing he can clutch up when needed.

Numbers just begin to tell the story with Wright, though. He tries to be fair to all people. He plays the game hard. He is old-school as he told the *New York Post*'s Steve Serby. "I idolize guys who play the game hard, play the right way, break up the double play, run over the catcher," Wright said. "To me an old-school type player is a guy that will do anything to win, will give up his body to win, will do the little things right to win."

Essentially, Wright was describing his own style of play and showing his passion for the game. "I've got plenty of friends who play baseball," he said, noting the flood of talent from Virginia that is in the major leagues and the friends he has made throughout the game through the years, "but when I put that uniform on, I'll be the first one to run 'em over at the plate. I'll be the first to take them out at second."

His definition of an MVP, he said, is the follow-

Giants pitcher Kevin Correia steps off the mound as David Wright rounds the bases after hitting an eighth-inning solo home run, Wright's second in the game.

ing: "A guy that puts winning before anything else; a guy that doesn't care about the statistics; a guy that I want up there in the clutch; a guy that when the game's on the line I want the ball to be hit to him; a guy that is the first one to get up and congratulate a teammate when he's 4-for-4 or 0-for-4."

In this 'Look at me' world those are important words, the kind of words that every Little Leaguer should read. Wright was taught the right way to play from his parents and coaches.

Although he does point out one critical coaching mistake his father made in Little League when he put David, who usually played shortstop, out in the outfield.

"I was one of the younger kids on the team," Wright said as he shot a knowing smile at his father. "My dad said I wasn't good enough to play the infield. Now I play third for the Mets."

Recalled Rhon, "He let me know in no uncertain terms he was not happy about it."

"That's why," Wright then tells his dad, "you were not the coach the next year...He was fired because of it and banned from all Tidewater-area coaching for that move."

The two laugh at the story. Rhon Wright said his son learned his values early. "David understood the importance of a good education and hard work and I think that carries into the ballfield. He may not be the most athletic, but he works as hard as he possibly can to get better."

This kind of hard work: As he got older and darkness would fall on the country ballfields near his home, David would position his car near the field with the high beams on to take extra grounders and play pepper, a trick he learned from Cuddyer.

David Wright would run out of daylight, but not the desire to be the best he could be. All that work

has paid off in so many ways. Wright is becoming one of the more popular athletes on the endorsement circuit. Wilson signed Wright to a five-year contract before the season because the glove manufacturer wanted to make Wright their Derek Jeter. Wilson produced a David Wright signature model glove. Wright always wanted his own glove because of his hero Cal Ripken Jr.

"As a kid that was a huge thrill for me, walking into a Modell's and picking out a Cal Ripken Jr. signature glove," Wright said. "It's cool to have my own glove. I'm excited."

He smiled and added, "I'm really not that good. I'm fooling somebody."

Wright has created the David Wright Foundation and has enlisted the help of other New York athletes like the Knicks' Channing Frye. "I want to get the foundation going in the same direction as Derek Jeter's Turn 2 Foundation," Wright said. "That's the goal. I just think it's awesome to give these groups the checks that they need."

Even though he signed that big deal and is set for life, you get the feeling Wright would play for free if he had to because the game means that much to him. Where else could Wright be having so much fun?

Wright made the catch of the 2005 season, when he snagged Brian Giles' pop fly with a running, over the shoulder grab, at Petco Park in San Diego.

Describing the play to Letterman, Wright noted, "I was listening to my voice mails after the game and everybody is saying, 'Great catch!' This and that, I get to a voice mail from my brothers and, you know, I made 23-24 errors last year, which is a lot, and they said, 'It's a good thing I didn't try to use my glove or I probably would have dropped it.' "

Don't expect David Wright to drop the ball for the Mets. ●

David Wright celebrates with on-deck batter Michael Tucker as Wright scores on Jose Valentin's two-run, seventh-inning single off San Diego Padres reliever Doug Brocail.

Magic Moments: May
The Mets Maintain Momentum

Life was so good for the Mets that even Victor Zambrano felt good about himself after his first start in May.

After tying a franchise record with 16 victories in April, the Mets started the first day of May right where they left off the previous month by registering another one-run victory, this time a 2-1 win over the Washington Nationals.

The Mets had gotten off to the kind of start they needed to make the National League East and New York take notice. There was more than Yankees-Red Sox. Attention was finally coming the Mets' way.

One-run victories were to be the calling card of this team. The difference between good and great is winning those one-run games. Winning those types of games has a lot to do with getting solid pitching, putting pressure on the defense and Willie Randolph's no-nonsense managing.

Randolph's goal from Day 1 was to get the Mets to be mentally tougher than the opponent so they could win these types of games. This victory marked Randolph's 100th managerial win.

This one-run win developed like so many others. The Mets' pitching kept it close and the Nationals made a key mistake. Reliever Gary Majewski made a throwing error in the bottom of the ninth that gave the Mets the gift victory. Majewski, trying to get an inning-ending double play, threw to second but the ball ticked off the glove of late-arriving shortstop Royce Clayton and went into centerfield, allowing Endy Chavez to score the winning run.

Walk-off errors produce the same results as walk-off hits. That error made a winner of Billy Wagner.

Zambrano was good on this day but he had not been able to do his job since being traded for phenom Scott Kazmir, one of the worst trades in Mets history.

With Zambrano, there always seems to be some kind of health issue. He came into May with a 9.64 ERA. Soon his season, and most likely his Mets career, came to an end due to serious arm problems.

Those who have kept a close eye on Zambrano, believe he is not the type of pitcher who could make the adjustments needed to succeed nor did he show the kind of fire in his belly needed to become a consistent major-league pitcher. You always got the feeling that Zambrano was just along for the ride.

Essentially, he is a lost cause, but in this game, Zambrano gave the Mets six good innings, allowing only five singles. Afterwards, he would tell reporters, "It's a good start for me. I feel more confident." Those turned out to be just more empty words from Zambrano.

Ironically, before the game, Randolph said the Mets would call up right-hander John Maine from Norfolk. After a slow start, the 6-foot-4 Maine would prove to be everything Zambrano was not on the mound. Maine, acquired from the Orioles in the trade for Kris Benson, had both ability and desire to be a successful pitcher and, like Carlos Delgado, keeps a record of his performance in a notebook.

David Wright watches the ball after he hit a game-winning single in the ninth inning against the New York Yankees. The Mets won, 7-6.

Lastings Milledge waves to the crowd before the Mets play the Arizona Diamondbacks. Milledge was called up after starting rightfielder Xavier Nady was placed on the disabled list following an appendectomy earlier in the day.

***

It's not just about talent. It's about knowledge, too.

Fourteen years of division championships for the Braves. Fourteen innings until the Mets broke through against Atlanta for an 8-7 victory on Cinco de Mayo. Funny, how it all works out.

To earn this win the Mets had to overcome a four-run deficit in the seventh. They had to get past Billy Wagner surrendering a pinch-hit home run to Wilson Betemit in the 11th. Cliff Floyd tied the score with a home run of his own in the bottom of the inning and then three innings later David (Walk-off) Wright doubled to win it and end the four-hour, 47-minute affair.

These kinds of wild wins were becoming routine for the Mets, and Willie Randolph, who usually doesn't get worked up about too much, even said, "This was as bizarre as they get."

That's the way life is with the find-a-way-to-win Mets. The roller coaster continued. Thrills everywhere you turn. The season was only a month old, but it was already clear that these were not your father's Braves. This Bobby Cox' crew does not have the pitching that was the hallmark of all the post-season Braves teams. These are the stumbling, bumbling Braves and the Mets were more than happy to give a karate chop after taking so many tomahawk chops from them.

Wright's double marked the third walk-off hit by the Mets in a week. Big Papi would be proud. And the youngest Mets were making their presence felt. Not only did Cox have to watch Wright beat him, but Cox gave Jose Reyes the first intentional walk of his career in the ninth, avoiding Reyes who was 5-for-5 at the time.

Even though Wagner was off to a struggling start, blowing three of his first 10 save opportunities and had given up a go-ahead home run in this game, the Mets were finding ways to weather the storm. Wagner got a lift from his teammates, prompting him to note, "It's a team game."

It sure is and the Mets were finally looking like the better team than the Braves. It was about time.

***

Time to take a deep breath Mets fans. Just like David Wright did in one of the most critical at-bats of the month for the team.

At 23, Wright is realizing every time he goes out on the field, it's a learning experience. On May 19 in the first game of the Subway Series with the Yankees, Wright had one great learning experience.

Two days earlier Wright got up in a key situation against the Cardinals' Jason Isringhausen. The bases

Willie Randolph embraces starting pitcher Alay Soler, a Cuban defector and Mets rookie who overcame a three-run deficit in the first inning in his major league debut as the Mets defeated the Phillies 5-4.

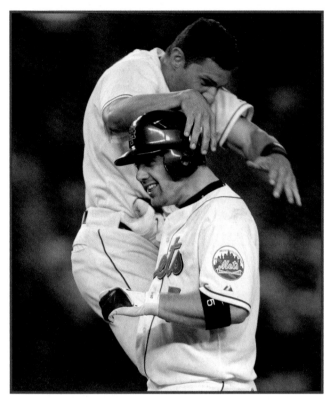

David Wright is congratulated by Jose Valentin after hitting a game-winning single against the Yankees during the ninth inning of their game.

were loaded. Wright looked at the situation and felt his body tighten. Isringhausen had Wright right where he wanted him and a few cut fastballs later, struck out the young slugger.

The great thing about baseball is there are so many games, so many learning experiences, so many second chances. Wright's came against the Yankees on this night. He learned from his mistake and told himself: "Don't tighten up. Stay relaxed. Relax your hands. Let it flow."

To do all that, the first thing Wright did was take a deep breath, and then another. "When you take deep breaths, it relaxes you," Wright would say later. "That's what I did against the Yankees. I didn't do that against the Cardinals."

Wright was facing Mariano Rivera and his new breathing technique worked perfectly. Wright lashed a booming shot to center that scored Paul Lo Duca to give the Mets a 7-6 victory. As Wright hit the ball, he bounced along the first base line, trying to coax the ball over the head of Johnny Damon. It worked.

It is that kind of enthusiasm that makes Wright such a special player. He is fun to watch. Like the All-American boy next door, it's easy for fans to root for him. "I was just hoping that the ball would make it over Johnny's head," Wright said. "It seemed to be up there forever. It's a great feeling to have another chance at it."

Another walk-off victory, this time in a game the Mets trailed Randy Johnson, 4-0.

That one hit, that one win showed that New York is no longer just a Yankee town. The Mets were making noise. They were becoming the life of the party. The night also featured an unbelievable performance by Billy Wagner, who struck out the side on 12 pitches in the ninth. Wagner was the winner in this "Enter Sandman" battle between himself and Rivera.

The Mets were thrilled, not only because they came away with another one-run victory, not only because they beat the Yankees, but also because Wright had learned a most valuable lesson.

As Willie Randolph said in the post-game press conference: "We talk to our young kids all the time about making adjustments. He made the adjustment. It's easy to forget that he's still just a baby in a lot of ways."

Wright's heroics would not have been possible if not for another tremendous night of work by the bullpen. Wagner did his thing in the ninth and Aaron Heilman was terrific setting him up, retiring all nine Yankees hitters he faced. Heilman is so effective that even though the Mets have a need for another starter, they cannot afford to move Heilman out of his setup role.

Baseball is a game of roles and Heilman's reliever

Carlos Beltran follows the trajectory of his ball after hitting a three-run home run during the first inning against the Yankees.

Paul Lo Duca goes airborne after making the out at the plate on Philadelphia Phillies' Chase Utley in the third inning. Steve Trachsel made the throw to LoDuca for the out on an infield grounder by Shane Victorino.

role is best for the team right now.

A lesser pitcher may have cracked. Billy Wagner blew a four-run lead to the Yankees a day earlier and here he was, called on once again on May 21. Wagner didn't fail this time, saving the 4-3 victory, giving the Mets two of the three games in the Subway Series.

The Mets continued to pass every test thrown their way this young season.

Wagner showed his toughness, telling a sea of reporters after the game, "I felt like I had a lot to prove to my teammates and prove to this city that one tough outing ain't going to break me."

Wagner got over his bad outing by going to the movies after Saturday's blowup, taking his wife Sarah to see *The DaVinci Code*. Relievers have to have short memories.

Willie Randolph made the right move again by going right back to Wagner, not allowing the bad taste of Saturday to linger too long. Wagner was pumped because this was his first taste of the Subway Series and he loved every minute of it.

One tough loss was not going to break the Mets, either. This bounce-back win put the Mets at 26-17 and gave them a better record than the 24-18 Yankees. The Mets were on their way to a special season that even the Yankees could admire.

The Yankees failed in 15 of the 17 attempts they had with runners in scoring position, one of the biggest failures of the night came when Duaner Sanchez got Alex Rodriguez to hit into an inning-ending double-play in the eighth.

This was a win the Mets had to have because it gave them the first series between the rivals and it also gave them breathing room with the second-place Phillies coming to town.

Tom Glavine was the winning pitcher, saying, "It's hard not to get amped up for the Yankees. They are what they are."

And the Mets are what they are--a team that is to be reckoned with, a team that would give the

David Wright is congratulated by teammates after a game-winning hit.

David Wright reacts after coming though in the clutch with a key hit against the Yankees.

The back-to-back blasts stunned Small and the Yankees, but that's what these Mets have been doing all season. If an opponent makes a mistake, the Mets make the most if it. That's how they make their magic.

***

Good teams forge comeback victories. Of the Mets' first 27 wins of the 2006 season, 11 were of the drama-filled, comeback variety. The amazing 9-8 victory over the Phillies on May 23 was just such a win...only this game went much deeper into the night. The Mets came back from a four-run deficit and a three-run deficit to win. They never quit.

It took 16 innings and a numbing five hours and 22 minutes before this game was decided by a Carlos Beltran walk-off home run. When Beltran touched home it was 12:33 in the morning. This was the longest game the Mets had played since a 7-5 loss to Houston on June 16, 1995.

David Wright put the night into perspective, saying, "If you're going to play 16 innings, you better win." Noted Willie Randolph, "You use all your players and play a gut-wrenching game like that, you have to win those games."

The home run was yet another sign that Beltran had put the disappointing 2005 season behind him. When Beltran was asked after the game if this was his best moment as a Met, he told *Newsday*, "Hasn't come yet. When we win the World Series, that will be my best moment as a Met."

This was the opening game of the series. The Mets had won the first game of every series they had played at home this season. That is how you wind up with a home record of 18-9 in April and May. They've made a statement each of those opening games.

You can't produce these kinds of victories in extra innings without big performances from the bullpen and the Mets were getting tremendous efforts from the pen, including Duaner Sanchez, whose ERA

Yankees a run for their money. This was another crazy game where the Mets scored all four of their runs in one inning, attacking Aaron Small in the fourth. In that inning, the Yankees saw the difference a Carlos Delgado can make to a lineup as Delgado crushed a three-run home run.

Then David Wright followed with another homer, a monumental blast, traveling 445 feet. Wright turned on a high fastball. He was proving to opponents that he could take the ball away and drive it right-center or turn on the inside pitch and send it for a ride to left. Delgado was impressed, noting "I'm a big fan of home runs. That was a nice one."

Kazuo Matsui and the Yankees' Derek Jeter look toward first after Alex Rodriguez grounded into an eighth-inning double play in the Mets' 4-3 win over the Yankees.

Jose Reyes watches the flight of his RBI single against the Arizona Diamondbacks during the ninth inning.

together one of their best performances of the season, beating the Diamondbacks, 1-0 at Shea in 13 innings, winning on an Endy Chavez RBI-single over a drawn-in infield. That hit scored Jose Valentin, who lashed a leadoff double.

This was a premier pitching matchup with Pedro Martinez going against Brandon Webb. It also was another example of Willie Randolph using his entire roster.

The victory marked the Mets' 16th one-run victory of the season, four more than anyone else. The only downside for the Mets in the month was that Martinez, who made six starts in May, did not register a win, marking the first month in his career where he had a least five starts and did not get a victory, according to the Elias Sports Bureau.

The team won, though, and that's what mattered, said Martinez, who pitched eight scoreless innings. "I know I'm going to win a lot more games," he offered.

dropped to 1.84.

The extra bullpen pieces, Chad Bradford and Darren Oliver, continued to make major contributions as well. Omar Minaya wanted to rebuild the bullpen in the off-season and he did just that. As Randolph said, you use all your players. Especially when you play 16 innings.

All the pieces were beginning to fit perfectly.

On the final game of the month, the Mets put

So were the Mets. Especially since Randolph made one of the key decisions of the season, inserting Valentin at second for the fourth straight game. As the season progressed, that move proved to be huge. In those four starts, Valentin was 7-for-16 with two home runs and six RBI, filling the one huge hole the Mets had because Kaz Matsui was not getting the job done.

"Championship teams have to win games like this," Valentin said of the victory. And the Mets did just that, which helped to make May one memorable month in New York. ●

David Wright swings for the fences in a game against the Yankees.

Magic Moments: June

The Form Of A Winner Takes Shape

The third Sunday of the month was Father's Day. In some ways, Mets fans could thank Omar Minaya's father Theodore for the team's success. Theodore taught his son many valuable lessons.

Minaya grew up in Queens with two sisters. "My father, who has since passed away, always encouraged us to shoot for the stars, don't be afraid to take risks," Minaya said, explaining his father's philosophy on life. "He trusted us, he was a disciplinarian but he also wasn't afraid to let us go a little bit. He taught us to do the right thing and that has stayed with me all these years."

The Mets continued to do the right thing in June because they came together as a team and their young players David Wright and Jose Reyes blossomed while Carlos Beltran looked like the 2004 playoff monster he was with Houston.

Jose Valentin also solidified his spot at second. He had come all the way back from a knee injury he suffered in a collision at home plate in May of 2005 with the Dodgers.

Second base had been a problem for the Mets ever since the arrival of shortstop Kaz Matsui. That signing forced the Mets to make one of the dumbest decisions any club has ever made.

Matsui was handed the shortstop position while Reyes was passed off as a second baseman, something he clearly wasn't. Matsui was eventually placed at second and Reyes was given his rightful position, short-

stop. Matsui couldn't handle second and the Mets were not comfortable with him at that spot.

For years the Mets thought they could simply flip positions on players. Remember when Roger Cedeno was going to be a centerfielder? Or Mike Piazza was going to be a first baseman? Same thing for Reyes going from short to second.

In spring training, Willie Randolph hinted that second was a position in flux, saying, "Sometimes you can't always get the guy you want. You go with what you have and try to transform their game a little bit to fit what you are. I love Craig Counsell but he's not here. You try to make do with what you have."

The Mets couldn't make do with Matsui, who was traded to the Colorado Rockies on June 9, along with $4.5 million for utility man Eli Marrero. That deal put an end to one of the most disappointing free-agent signings in Mets' history.

The Mets came together this month on the road. An 11-day trip to Los Angeles, Arizona and Philadelphia produced a 9-1 record. With summer approaching, the Mets were the hottest team in the city. "It's all about winning," noted Randolph. "Everyone loves a winner, fans get behind you when you do well. That's the bottom line. This is an exciting club."

On June 4, the day before the Mets played in Los Angeles, rookie Lastings Milledge had his happiest moment in his brief time as a Met, slugging a two-out, 10th-inning home run against Armando Benitez, who

David Wright hits his second home run during the 5th inning of a game against the Cincinnati Reds.

Jose Reyes congratulates Pedro Martinez after Martinez completed six innings in the Mets' 6-2 win.

was now the Giants' problem, to tie the wild game, 6-6. That home run followed a solo shot by Jose Valentin. Milledge had a two-run double earlier in the game so he was one excited 21-year-old. As he went back out to right field for the top of the 11th, Milledge took a route along the stands to joyfully high-five dozens of fans.

This was his New York coming-out party. It was nothing more than a rookie showing excitement but Milledge was hammered by critics for the high-fives, especially since the Mets lost the game, 7-6 in the 12th inning. Willie Randolph had a talk with Milledge about baseball etiquette after the game.

"It will not happen again," the manager promised.

"I honestly wasn't showing anyone up," Milledge

Lastings Milledge swings for a double in a game against the San Francisco Giants.

would tell reporters later. "It was a rookie mistake."

Milledge was called to the majors ahead of schedule because right-fielder Xavier Nady had to undergo an appendectomy one week earlier.

As *New York Post* columnist Mike Vaccaro said of Milledge's mistake: "If the worst we'll ever say about Milledge is that he got a little too excited after his first signature moment as a major leaguer, then Milledge will have lived a long and prosperous baseball life."

Indeed.

The Mets had let one game get away, Milledge was taking the heat, it was the perfect time to travel 3,000 miles to LA.

***

The Dodgers were a team in transition. Like Minaya, they were being run by an excellent baseball man, Ned Colletti, who came over from the archrival Giants. And like Minaya, Colletti learned valuable lessons from his father, the most important, the value of hard work.

He remembers being sent to Joe & Al's Delicatessen every week in Franklin Park, Ill. "On Sundays I'd walk up and buy five slices of boiled ham," Colletti recalled. Those five slices of meat would become a week's worth of lunch-time sandwiches for his father, Ned Sr., one slice a day for his blue-collar job at Motorola.

There was no garage to park the car at their tiny home, so, in the dead of winter, Ned. Sr. would get up in the middle of the night and start the car and let it run for 15 minutes so the battery would not go dead from the cold. "If my father didn't go to work, he didn't get paid," Colletti explained.

"All that taught me to take nothing for granted, to cherish every day and to work as hard as you can work to support your family."

With that kind of nose-to-the-grindstone attitude, it would only be a matter of time before the Dodgers turned it around, but it wasn't going to be the night of June 5.

The Mets blasted two home runs, got a solid effort from rookie pitcher Alay Soler and beat L.A., 4-1 before 34,420 at Dodger Stadium. Jose Reyes, showing he had a little Rickey Henderson in him, clubbed a leadoff home run, and Carlos Delgado, who would struggle most of the year to find his hitting groove, snapped a two-week homerless streak with a two-run shot of his own in the inning.

Delgado, who keeps it simple, told reporters his swing was "much better" the last few days. After dropping two of three to the Giants at home, the Mets were feeling much better, too.

Milledge continued his hot-hitting too, knocking in the Mets' final run with a single in the sixth and he also seemed not to care what anybody thought about his high-five extravaganza, saying, "I decided to show the fans some love."

***

Sometimes you throw things against a wall just to see what sticks. That's what Omar Minaya decided to do in his never-ending search for starting pitching.

One of the pitchers that stuck was ex-Yankee Orlando Hernandez, the ageless wonder. Who knows how old El Duque really is, but he can still pitch. Hernandez showed that on June 8, coming up with a huge performance against the team the Mets acquired him from, the Arizona Diamondbacks. Of course, El Duque is always more effective when he can show up the team that got rid of him.

When El Duque was with the Yankees he showed a penchant for pitching the big game and that's why Minaya took a shot at him. He did not disappoint on this night, pitching a complete game, in a 7-1 victory at Chase Field.

You just knew it was going to be a special year when things like this happened. Minaya could probably sign Nolan Ryan for a day and get a complete game out of him.

Then again, the Mets have a comfort zone against the D-Backs. Perhaps it goes back to the 1999 play-

Chris Woodward looks toward first base along with Cincinnati Reds' Ryan Freel, who was out when Felipe Lopez hit into a double play.

David Wright greets teammates Carlos Beltran and Eli Marrero at the plate as Orioles catcher Javy Lopez stands behind the celebrating Mets after Wright hit a fifth-inning grand slam off Orioles pitcher Adam Loewen.

offs when the Mets beat Arizona in the Division Series in four games, the final victory coming on Todd Pratt's walk-off home run to give John Franco his first post-season victory.

Hernandez' win was the Mets' fifth straight at Chase Field and in those games the Mets outscored Arizona 46-8. Hernandez was so amazingly good in a place he had pitched so poorly when he was a mem-ber of the D-Backs. In his six starts at home he was 0-3 with an 8.16 ERA for Arizona, yet none of that mattered. When El Duque puts New York on his chest, he becomes a different pitcher.

Catcher Paul Lo Duca marveled at Hernandez' control, telling reporters that Hernandez threw his curve ball wherever he wanted, whenever he wanted. That sounds much like the El Duque the Yankees knew before he ran into a series of shoulder woes.

The *New York Post* headline over Mark Hale's game story said it all: "No Fluque". As for that complete game performance, Hernandez told Hale, "It's my responsibility ever day when I go out to the mound."

Ramon Castro points as he crosses the plate in a win against the Orioles.

Orioles catcher Javy Lopez can't make the tag as David Wright slides safely into home.

Hernandez certainly had something to prove. The complete game was his first since Sept. 16, 2000, when he was a Yankee, prompting pitching coach Rick Peterson to note, "That's signature El Duque."

No Fluque at all. The win also moved the Mets 13 games above .500 for the first time this season. El Duque was one of George Steinbrenner's favorite Yankees because of his gutsy approach to pitching. Minaya took a flyer on him and something stuck.

***

On the fifth day of the trip, it was Carlos Times Two. Carlos Beltran and Carlos Delgado each hit two home runs in the desert on June 9 to lead the Mets to a 10-6 win over Arizona.

Delgado said his swing was much better and on this night he showed it. Beltran has been a totally different player all year with Delgado protecting him in the lineup. Just as important, Beltran is healthy.

Carlos & Carlos make the Mets a most dangerous team.

"We're capable of that type of offense," Willie Randolph told reporters. "I don't think we've scratched the surface of our offense."

For opponents, that's one frightening thought and that's why as you traveled around baseball, you heard again and again that the Mets' lineup was the most feared in the National League.

Chase Field is aptly named because the balls can fly out of there and the Mets' hitters were happy to be playing four games in such a friendly ballpark to be followed up by three games in Philadelphia. That's a week that could get any slumping hitter out of a rut.

While they were hitting home runs on this day, the Mets dumped some excess baggage off on the Colorado Rockies, sending Kaz Matsui away for utility man Eli Marrero. So much for the $20.1 million signing that was to be the Mets answer to the Yankees

Heath Bell reacts after a double play against the Cincinnati Reds.

signing of Hideki Matsui.

Matsui was the No. 1 target of the Mets boo birds at Shea Stadium, making it difficult for him to ever get it together. Hitting coach Rick Down told John Delcos of the *Journal News*, "I don't know if (Matsui) ever played with a lot of confidence. Personally, I don't know how a player can show his face on the field when he's getting booed like that. He didn't perform well and he didn't handle it well. Every at-bat was a life-and-death thing. Confidence is such an elusive thing and he didn't have it."

No he didn't. Some trades are salary dumps. This was a Kaz dump, the Mets also had to give $4.6 million to Colorado. Randolph & Co. liked the feel of their team with Jose Valentin at second and although Matsui was never a problem, he worked hard and tried to be the best player he could be--he never really fit in with the kind of club that Minaya was trying to mold. As a result, Matsui also understood the need for a change of scenery and waived his no-trade clause.

***

Life couldn't be better for the Mets. No one has had this much fun on a road trip since the lads from *Animal House* decided to get off campus.

The Mets completed a four-game sweep of the Diamondbacks at Chase Field with a 15-2 thumping on June 11. The tone for the month had been set in the desert and the Mets were flying high. They were flexing their muscles and loving every minute of it. The Braves were already 10 games behind and the Phillies were next in the Mets sights, prompting winning pitcher Pedro Martinez to tell reporters after the slaughter, "If I was the other team, I'd be worried right now."

No worries, mate, for the Mets.

Hitters talk about how contagious it can all become when one player after another starts swinging a hot bat.

The same goes for pitching. When starters start to roll, they try to outdo one another so they have something else to talk about on the golf course. The Mets

were getting great pitching and hitting on the trip.

No hitter was hotter than Carlos Beltran, who knows what it's like to get hot in a series. Beltran lashed nine hits in 17 at-bats in the Arizona series. He drove in 10 runs in the four games and bashed three doubles and three home runs. That's sick.

Success was carrying over month to month. The end of one month would highlight what was to come the next and the Mets' 6-2 win over the Reds at Shea on June 22 really put David Wright in the spotlight, a spotlight that would shine bright in July in Pittsburgh at the All-Star Game.

Wright blasted two home runs in back-to-back innings on this hazy day as he made a winner out of Martinez. Martinez knows his sluggers. David Ortiz and Manny Ramirez are two of his best friends in the game so when he was asked about what Wright was accomplishing this season, Martinez, whose baseball IQ is off the charts, said of the young third baseman, "MVP so far. That kid has done it all."

"He's been phenomenal," added Willie Randolph.

And when your team is 45-27 and running away with the division, MVP talk is not cheap.

Wright had to claw his way up into Willie Randolph's lineup. Randolph makes players earn their position in the lineup and Wright was no exception. He gradually moved up his rookie year and now Randolph was occasionally batting him fourth. In 69 at-bats in that spot he was batting a robust .435.

Martinez was appreciative of the offense because this marked the time of year where he begins to wear down. The All-Star break could not come quick enough for Pedro. The Mets had built themselves a 10-game lead in the division. Wright and Jose Reyes were on fire. Reyes had hit for the cycle the previous game and started this one off with a single and stole second and third.

With Reyes and Wright leading the way, and chants of MVP in the air, the Mets were set to have a super summer. ●

Julio Franco loses the bat, the first of two flying bats during his pinch-hit at-bat against the Phillies. Franco got a single and stole second base in the inning.

Doing It His Way

The Enigmatic Martinez Delivers Swagger & Substance

Watching Pedro Martinez pitch is watching an artist work. Each pitch is another brush stroke. Each pitch sets up the next. Each inning builds for the following inning. Precision and care are what he is all about on the mound.

And like a true artist, Pedro is unpredictable.

His feel for the game is remarkable. After getting off to a great start in 2006, Martinez was out of the rotation for an extended period of time in the middle of the season due to injuries and was missed in many ways.

It's not just about performance with Pedro; it's about charisma, too. When Pedro is not pitching, not performing, the Mets lose a little of the pizazz that makes them so endearing. They become pretty ordinary, and they did just that putting up a 13-11 record during his absence.

"Pedro is remarkable," third baseman David Wright told reporters when Pedro returned from the aches and pains of his midseason. "He's the anchor of this staff. He's so important. We need a healthy Pedro to get where we want to be. There's energy and an aura about him that not too many pitchers have. So I think that rubs off on the rest of the clubhouse when you have Pedro Martinez pitching."

It rubs off on his teammates. Pedro truly is the life of the Mets' party. That's why the Mets and Omar Minaya signed him to a four-year, $53 million contract after the 2004 season. Omar saw what Pedro could do for them on the mound and in the clubhouse.

New Yorkers catch on quickly. In no time at all they fell in love with Pedro. They realized that this was not the bully they saw toss Don Zimmer to the ground. They realized Pedro was a caring individual and a great teammate, someone who knew how to have fun in the clubhouse and on the field.

Pedro is Broadway all the way. In no time at all he was accepted for who he was, not rejected because he was once the pitching leader of the hated Red Sox. The Mets fans also quickly learned that a Pedro Martinez start brings life to Shea Stadium, the same kind of energy that was there when golden boy Tom Seaver started or when phenom Dwight Gooden let loose with his laser arm.

Each moment matters when Pedro is on the mound. You never know what's going to happen. He might tiptoe through the sprinklers one minute, bow to Carlos Beltran after a great catch or be swinging a plastic rally Mets bat to get the team going. He has Hall of Fame stuff and a carefree Little League attitude, all rolled into one.

And yes, when he is on the mound, more than likely, he is making the perfect pitch. Minaya dreamed it would be like this when he signed the free agent, stunning the baseball world because less than a month before the signing, Pedro and the Red Sox became World Champions.

Minaya reasoned that Pedro would win over the Big Apple in no time. There was just too much talent there not to love Pedro, too much personality in that

Pedro Martinez strikes a classicly defiant pose as he talks to fans from the dugout during a game against the Los Angeles Dodgers.

Pedro Martinez bears down during the second inning of a game against the Arizona Diamondbacks.

wiry body. Too many wins in that golden right arm, an arm that Pedro closely monitored since suffering shoulder problems in 2001 that limited him to 116.2 innings pitched that season.

"Pedro is not only a Hall of Fame pitcher," Minaya said of New York's love affair with Pedro. "He's a personality. New Yorkers, we want personality."

In Pedro, they got that and much more.

Martinez showed up at Shea with three Cy Young Awards under his belt and a lifetime record of 182-76. Most of all, New Yorkers love winners and Pedro is just that. His first year with the Mets, he compiled a 15-8 record with a 2.82 ERA. He third 20-win season was a possibility if he had gotten a little more help from the bullpen, but Pedro never complained about any of that.

He showed he was a classy teammate and that was another reason for the fans to cheer him. So when Martinez showed up at spring training early in 2006, his aching big toe was the big story, especially since the Knicks were going through one of the most embarrassing years of their existence.

It was all Pedro, all the time.

When would the specially designed shoe arrive to Port St. Lucie? Would it fit? Would it help? Would Pedro be able to start the season in the rotation?

Pedro quickly answered all those questions and got

Pedro Martinez delivers a pitch in the first inning of a game against the Florida Marlins.

off to a 5-0 start with a 2.94 ERA by April 28. By midseason, Pedro had once again been named to another All-Star team, one of six Mets to be honored. But he couldn't pitch in Pittsburgh. He slipped and fell in the visiting clubhouse in Florida in late May and that aggravated a hip injury. It was that problem that kept him out of the All-Star Game. He was replaced by Roy Oswalt.

But anyone who really knows Pedro, knows that pitching in an All-Star Game at this stage of his career, puts too much of a burden on his shoulder. He needs the All-Star break to do just that, take a break and that's what he did in 2006. When you are 34, you have to make adjustments. While taking that break, Pedro came down with a bad case of food poisoning that also set him back.

The Mets had built a huge lead, however, and there was no need to rush back into the rotation. They kept that lead all summer and heading down the stretch, pitching coach Rick Peterson could map out a plan where Pedro would get his rest so that he would be strong going into October, when the Mets needed him most.

The secret to Pedro's success is his work ethic. In spring training, his workout regime takes seven hours, all done with the idea of strengthening his right shoulder. If you're a reporter and you need to talk to Pedro, you better get him before he heads to his workout or else you are in for a long day.

Pedro enjoys the give-and-take with the media, just as he enjoys every other aspect of the game. There are many times I've been at Pedro's locker and talked about gardening or world events.

Baseball is his job, it does not define him. Pedro also has a deep belief in himself, and is comfortable with his place in the world.

Most of all though, Pedro is a competitor and that's why to this day he remains upset with the Red Sox and GM Theo Epstein for not making more of an effort to re-sign him after the 2004 championship sea-son. Essentially, The Red Sox waved goodbye to Pedro and Derek Lowe and replaced them with David Wells and Matt Clement.

Red Sox fans have been in denial over the entire affair, but there is no disputing the numbers. With the Red Sox, Martinez posted a stunning 117-37 record. He compiled the best winning percentage in Sox history (minimum 100 decisions). That .760 winning percentage was 84 points better than runner-up Smokey Joe Wood (117-56, .676). That kind of production comes along once in a lifetime.

The Red Sox' loss was the Mets gain. The Boston pitching staff hasn't been the same since Pedro departed, missing his leadership and his winning ways.

Peterson, a deep thinker, knows what he has in Pedro anchoring his staff. "Pedro is a pitching genius," Peterson said. "The most important thing is how confident he is. When you're a pitcher like Pedro is, the expectations are always high, and they should be."

Bench coach Jerry Manuel said this about the ace: "There are some guys who once they lose their great stuff they can't adjust to lesser stuff, but not him. He's just beautiful to watch. When he's pitching, you take a front-row seat."

And enjoy the view as Pedro makes adjustments start-to-start, pitch-to-pitch.

Martinez believes in his stuff, everything from his fastball to his changeup. Never underestimate the power of his changeup. Asked where he would be without that pitch, Pedro said: "I'd probably still be in the bullpen."

That's where a young Pedro Martinez was when he was with the Dodgers. Then he mastered the changeup and his pitching world changed. The reason Pedro can throw his changeup with such precision is that his fingers are so long and flexible. In fact, Pedro is capable of bending his fingers backward to nearly his wrist. He is that double-jointed. That allows him to get extra spin on the ball, creating more movement.

Pedro Martinez locks onto his target in a game against the Philadelphia Phillies.

"I've seen him throw it seven straight times," explained Mets bullpen coach Guy Conti. No one knows Pedro better than Conti, who was in player development with the Dodgers when Pedro was a youngster. Conti's wife Jan helped teach Pedro English.

"Every day Pedro would learn a couple new words," Conti recalled. "He was always the nicest young man. He would help my wife carry the groceries. He was like family."

During his time away from the game, Pedro loves to garden. "I love to talk to my flowers," he said. "It helps them grow."

At home in the Dominican he is beloved because of the pitcher and person that he is, helping so many people. He quietly supplied the money for the building of Immaculate Conception Church back home and has helped build many homes for his countrymen. Martinez is always looking to help those who need help. He pitches and acts from the heart. "A lot of people who don't know Pedro, don't understand him," Minaya said. "He's a very giving teammate."

Pedro also is one of the smartest players in the game. Jason Varitek, Manny Ramirez, David Ortiz know the importance of Pedro. "Pedro is the guy who kept everything there going," Minaya says of Pedro's Boston days.

"I miss Pedro," Big Papi said.

Whenever Pedro pitches it's a show, but not just during the game.

The next time you are at the ballpark when Pedro is pitching, watch him warm up in the bullpen. He doesn't just loosen up like most pitchers. He is not just out there taking up space. He actually mimics the game, down to details like wiping his brow, taking his time to get the right feel for the baseball and pausing between pitches as he gazes into the stands to gather himself.

He is prepared. Every detail is checked. He is an artist at work.

Minaya and his baseball people love to watch Pedro work in his surgical manner. "You try to follow Pedro's pitch pattern, but you can't," Minaya explained. "You expect a fastball in, but you get a changeup away."

Only Pedro knows. That's the way it is. After all, this is Pedro's Show. This is now Pedro's Town and he will go down as one of the greatest pitchers of all time. Yankees third baseman Alex Rodriguez said of Martinez when he was a free agent: "I've been in the majors for 10 years, and for me the best pitcher I've seen is Pedro Martinez. He is a genius with the ball, has incredible discipline and knowledge of baseball. I love him and respect him a lot."

Martinez has a gift. He sees not only what is happening on the mound, but he can see what is going on around him. He has a sense of team that few players possess. When he first came to the Mets, he knew it was going to be an uphill climb, especially leaving a championship ballclub, coming to a rebuilding club. But there was hope. He had faith that better days would be ahead and he was willing to pay the price to help the Mets grow into a winning team.

He liked the Mets attitude. He loved Minaya's game plan for the future. He believed in it. He loved what he saw in young players David Wright and Jose Reyes. When the *Boston Globe*'s Gordon Edes came down to New York to do a story on Pedro his first year as a Met, Pedro put his new team in perspective, telling Edes: "This team, I think next year is going to be our year, when they start playing together and they get to know what to do, this is a team that's built for the future."

Pedro saw the future. He saw where the Mets were heading.

As Wright so aptly pointed out, though, for the Mets to get where they need to be, they need Pedro to lead the way.

Pedro Martinez is what winning is all about. ●

Pedro Martinez unleashes a filthy pitch in the first inning of a game against the Atlanta Braves.

Magic Moments: July

Mets Continue Their Remarkable Roll

Willie Randolph is one patient man. Back in 1976 he started his Yankee career 0-for-11. In his 12th at-bat, he homered off Hall of Famer Jim Palmer.

So he wasn't going to worry about a little stumble from his Mets in the last week of June and the first three days of July as the Mets dropped six of seven games. Why worry? The Pirates were in town.

Even though the Mets weren't playing their best--Randolph said the team was mentally tired--they were still good enough to beat the lowly Pirates, who came into Shea with the worst road record in baseball.

On July 4 the Mets needed a victory, and it didn't matter how they got it. For nine days the Mets got the chance to play in the American League East with interleague games against the Blue Jays, Red Sox and Yankees and that was a tough task. To make matters worse, Pedro Martinez was out with hip and toe woes

They opened a four-game series with the Pirates with a 10-run loss. They were officially slumping, having lost 11 of the last 17 games. "We haven't been playing the way we were used to playing," noted shortstop Jose Reyes.

But in typical 2006 Mets fashion, they came up big when they needed it, and scored three runs in the eighth inning to come away with a 7-6 victory over Pittsburgh to up their record to 49-34. In the process, though, they lost Cliff Floyd with a mild concussion after he collided with Reyes.

The Mets, though, have a way of turning negatives

into positives and Floyd's replacement, Endy Chavez supplied an RBI-double in the eighth. Chavez then came up with a tremendous slide at home to score on Xavier Nady's hit.

Randolph makes the most of his bench and that's part of the secret of his managing success. "Our bench guys look forward to contributing," Randolph told reporters. "I make it a practice of making sure they stay fresh, communicating with them daily to make sure they feel as much part of the team as the regular guys."

This win wasn't all about bench guys.

The Guy in the bullpen, Billy Wagner, came on to pick up his 300th save, only the 19th pitcher to reach that mark. "It means I'm getting old," Wagner said. Then he turned serious, telling reporters, "To come from where I've come from, 300 means a lot to me. It's special."

It did mean a lot to him. Wagner rarely shows emotion on the field, but after he locked this one up, he pumped his fist in celebration.

The win was the Mets 19th one-run victory of the season. Here's the other side of the coin. The one-run loss was the 25th of the season for the Pirates. There is a fine line between success and failure.

Taking advantage of the weak is what good teams do so the Mets went out the next night and jumped on Pittsburgh early, scoring five times in the first inning. That was good enough for Orlando Hernandez, who threw seven shutout innings for the 5-0 win and gave

Jose Valentin turns a double play as the Florida Marlins' Dan Uggla attempts to break it up during the first inning in the second game of a doubleheader. Valentin batted in seven of the Mets' 17 runs in their 17-3 victory.

Endy Chavez is ruled safe scoring on Xavier Nady's eighth inning two-run single for the go-ahead run in a Mets 7-6 come-from-behind victory over the Pittsburgh Pirates. Although it appeared that Pirates catcher made the tag, home plate umpire Angel Hernandez ruled in favor of the Mets.

the Mets their 50th victory of the season.

Hernandez had given the Mets just what they needed – over his last four starts his ERA was 3.18. The Mets won even though David Wright was given his second night off of the year. Randolph, knowing Wright would be busy in the upcoming All-Star Game, recognized Wright needed a rest.

Wright was now the face of the franchise. It was going to be his team for at least the next seven years. Interestingly enough, the former face of the franchise, Mike Piazza, was only an hour and a half ride away

from New York down in Philadelphia. His Padres were not arriving at Shea for another month, and Piazza admitted he was anxious for that time to come, curious at the reception he would receive.

"I just hope it doesn't take too much out of me," he said of his Shea homecoming. "I'm going to try and keep it together. Even now, I get so many positive letters from people wishing me the best. When I go back I want to say hi, but I also want to try and do my job and be a professional. I'll always enjoy going back there."

***

The Mets fans would show Piazza nothing but love in that series. Piazza admitted he missed the Mets even though he liked his new "beach bum" life.

"You don't spend eight years with a team and not miss people," Piazza said. "But it's good. I'm happy for the fans. A big investment has been put into the team

Willie Randolph congratulates closer Billy Wagner on his 300th save.

Jose Reyes, David Wright, Paul Lo Duca, Carlos Beltran, Tom Glavine and Pedro Martinez were all selected to be in the 2006 All-Star game.

and it's good to see it has finally paid off because there were some tough days there.

"It's nice there now, they're not always looking to one guy to carry the team."

Piazza had carried that offensive weight for so many years. Now that weight was distributed among Wright, Carlos Beltran, Jose Reyes, Carlos Delgado, Cliff Floyd, Paul Lo Duca and others.

"Once you take on a different role, it's kind of nice to watch other guys contribute," Piazza said.

Piazza also got to experience something new,

besides living near the beach in La Jolla, for the first time in his career he was being managed by a catcher, Bruce Bochy.

"Mike has no ego," Bochy said. "He's accomplished a lot in the game and is headed to the Hall of Fame but he's all about being a good teammate and winning.

Said Piazza, "Boch is unbelievable, he's the best. We just clicked off the bat and I love Willie (Randolph) too, he was great to me. The situations are a little different. Willie is a young manager, he's still going to learn."

The season was reaching its halfway point, but plenty of learning was still ahead for some of the youngest Mets.

With Pedro Martinez down there was an opening for

David Wright congratulates John Maine as they leave the field after Maine completed seven innings in a 1-0, 10-inning victory over the Cubs. Maine allowed no runs on three hits, struck out seven and allowed three walks in the outing.

Jose Reyes steals second on Chris Woodward's fifth-inning at-bat as Pittsburgh Pirates shortstop Jack Wilson reacts.

the minors.

So when Pelfry made his Mets debut in the second game of a doubleheader on June 8th, the 41,477 at Shea gave him a standing ovation. The Marlins had beaten young John Maine 3-2 in the first game, but in the second game the 22-year-old Pelfry notched his first major league win.

His new teammates gave him plenty of help as the Mets roughed up the Marlins, 17-3, and Pelfry lasted five innings, walked four batters and hit one.

When young pitchers get in the spotlight after so much buildup, they usually try too hard and wind up overthrowing. That's exactly what happened to Pelfry in his first major league start. "I was trying to throw the ball through the backstop," he told reporters.

He sure was. He also said he knew he could do better and would do better in the future. Mets fans were thrilled. They had gotten a glimpse of the future and another win in the process. Pelfry has the stuff to anchor the rotation for years to come because his fastball was consistently hitting 97-98, and here's the key: there is movement to his pitches.

All he needs is time to grow.

***

Another young Met was doing just that. David Wright was on a roll heading into the All-Star break where he would show the baseball world how much fun it is to watch him play.

When a player shows love for the game, it usually loves him right back. That's the way it is for Wright

Mike Pelfry in the rotation. The 6-foot-7 Pelfry was the Mets first-round selection in the 2005 draft and from the first day of spring training, Mets' brass loved what they saw of the right-hander.

The first thing you notice about him on the mound was that his legs seemed to stretch directly into his throwing arm and the action those legs generated was key to his success.

In 2005, Pelfry went 12-3 with a 1.93 ERA for Wichita State and posted a three-year mark of 33-7 with a 2.18 ERA, breaking Darren Dreifort's Shockers mark, which was 2.24. Mets fans are an optimistic lot and are good at keeping tabs on the club's prospects in

Billy Wagner grimmaces after beating the Yankees Derek Jeter to first base for the final out of the Mets' 8-3 win at Yankee Stadium.

Cliff Floyd leaves the game after suffering a mild concussion after colliding with shortstop Jose Reyes while the pair were fielding a fly ball against the Pittsburgh Pirates. Reyes made the catch for the out on the play.

and Jose Reyes. Wright headed into the break with style, belting a three-run home run in the eighth inning to lift the Mets to a 7-6 victory over the Marlins on June 9.

He left for Pittsburgh with a .316 average, 20 home runs and 74 RBI. Not a bad half-season of work.

"I think I'm heading in the right direction," Wright told reporters. "I've scuffled here and there, but I think that's a result of being young."

All that learning, Wright added, is "what makes the game so beautiful. You always have room for improvement."

With comments like that, how can the baseball world not love David Wright? Reyes was looking to have fun in Pittsburgh, too, but a headfirst slide into first base on Friday night put an end to that as Reyes suffered a cut to his left pinkie that took seven stitches to close.

"I'm disappointed," Reyes said. "I've learned my lesson. No more head-first slides into first."

Wright's 20th home run gave the Mets three players with at least that many. Carlos Beltran led the Mets with 25 and Carlos Delgado, despite his ups and downs, lashed 22. That marked the first time in New York history that one team had three players with at least 20 home runs at the break, according to the Elias Sports Bureau.

At the All-Star Game Wright made it clear how proud he was to be a Met, saying, "Everybody knows how I feel. I want to be a Met for a long, long time. When you play the game right, your day will come and I know that."

His financial day would come quicker than he thought.

***

Some things in baseball can't be explained. They just happen. You sit back and enjoy. Don't ask questions, just enjoy.

Such was the case on July 16 when the Mets erupted for 11 runs in the top of the sixth inning against the Cubs at Wrigley Field. The Mets hit two grand slams in the inning, one by Cliff Floyd, and the other by Carlos Beltran. The merry-go-round of runners was spinning so fast that Beltran thought there were only two runners on base when he hit his grand slam. He never saw the runner at third. He didn't realize the bases were loaded until he exchanged high-fives with his teammates at home plate.

This was an E-Z Pass inning for the Mets, another magical moment in a magical season. The Mets were

Jose Valentin belts a two-out 10th inning game-winning RBI single off pitcher Glendon Rusch to give the Mets a 1-0 victory over the Chicago Cubs.

grand slam happy and this marked their third and fourth of the season, matching last year's total and it was the first time they had ever hit two grand slams in a game, let alone an inning. This was only the seventh time in major league history that one club had hit two grand slams in an inning.

There's much more: The 11-run inning was the biggest inning in club history and it marked the first time the Cubs had ever surrendered two grand slams in an inning. Perhaps that's why Cubs manager Dusty Baker was so frustrated. It didn't help that Todd Walker's error made eight of the 11 runs unearned.

Floyd, who battled assorted injuries, all season, finally had his golden moment and it came in front of his hometown fans as he hit two home runs on the day. He told reporters when he hit his grand slam, "It felt like the whole planet fell off my shoulders."

Entering a free agent year, the weight is heavy. Floyd bashed 34 home runs in 2005 and this performance gave him nine on the season.

Grand slams were becoming a way of life for the Mets. Jose Valentin blasted one on July 21 that led the Mets to a 7-0 win over the Astros at Shea. The star of the game, though, was young John Maine, who pitched the complete-game shutout for his first win as a Met.

This is the way it's going for the Mets. Maine wasn't even supposed to pitch on this night. He got his chance because of a pre-game rain delay that shut down Orlando Hernandez. Willie Randolph didn't want to put El Duque through another start and stop performance after two previous starts where he had to deal with the elements. Rain and Maine, though, proved to be a great combination for the Mets.

Maine, 25, surrendered only four hits as he became the ray of light in the Kris Benson trade. Maine said he didn't know he was going to pitch until the last minute. "It didn't give me much of a chance to think of the hitters," Maine said. "I think that was best." Omar Minaya was shopping for a starting pitcher with the trade deadline approaching. One may have

popped up out of nowhere for him.

***

Pedro Martinez hadn't been on the mound in a month. His last win came on June 22. So when the first four Atlanta batters reached and scored on him on July 28 at Turner Field, it looked bleak.

In what was to be an up and down season for Martinez, filled with nagging injuries, the veteran found a way to get it together and beat the Braves, 6-4. "I'm proud of what I did tonight," Martinez told reporters. "I kept my team in the game."

He also put Atlanta a full 13 games back of the Mets.

Before that first game of the series, there was a lot of Brave talk about Atlanta still being in the race, but that's all it was, talk. This race is over. The Mets could now use the rest of the year to get their pitching in order for the playoffs and that meant making sure Pedro is right. There were more injuries ahead for Pedro, a strained right calf would knock him out in Philadelphia on Aug. 14.

The Mets had found a way to take care of business in the first four months of the season. Carlos Beltran was on fire in July. The centerfielder smacked 10 home runs and drove in 32 runs. Included in that explosion were three grand slams.

Beltran said it felt like the 2004 post-season all over again. And then came the words that every Mets fan wanted to hear: "My confidence is high now like it was then."

As the month came to a close the Mets as a team were sky-high, despite the loss of set-up man Duaner Sanchez, who was injured in a cab accident in Miami. When reporters asked Willie Randolph about the post-season, remember, they are paid to look ahead, the manager said, "Playoffs? C'mon, playoffs already? I'm talking about just getting my team through August."

He had to say that. Even though it was the heat of summer, you could be sure the Mets were thinking about crisp October nights. ●

Paul Lo Duca smacks a double down the left-field line.

Magic Moments: August
Turning Fantasy Into Reality

Omar Minaya's strength is that he can think short-term and long-term at the same time. So while the GM was pulling off the trade deadline deal with Pittsburgh to get Roberto Hernandez back to help the bullpen after the Duaner Sanchez cab accident, he was also moving forward on signing Jose Reyes to a four-year, $23.25 million contract.

Three days later, Minaya locked up David Wright to a six-year, $55 million contract. The Mets beat the Phillies, 8-1, that day, so they won across the board. The present and future were coming together in perfect fashion.

"To be able to get David Wright and Jose Reyes signed, it's a very special week for the Mets," Minaya said, adding with a smile that Mets fans would take comfort in the knowledge that they could buy a Reyes or Wright jersey and know they could wear it for a long, long time.

A shortstop like Reyes and a third baseman like Wright come along once in a GM's lifetime. Minaya knew he had to make the most of the situation and he did. The days of losing young studs like Scott Kazmir are done.

The Mets stumbled early in the month as they tried to overcome the loss of Sanchez, who was injured on July 31, hours after the Mets completed a sweep of the Braves in Atlanta. Aaron Heilman was given the job of eighth-inning bridge worker and rolled out two straight 1-2-3 performances, but then faltered with his third straight day of work in a 4-1 loss to the Marlins in Miami.

Heilman, who would rather be a starter, was challenged by Minaya and Willie Randolph to pick up the slack and he did just that in a 4-3 win over the Phillies on August 5.

The Mets had time to get their bullpen together. There was the addition of Hernandez and they continued to get good outings from Chad Bradford and Darren Oliver to go along with Heilman's work and closer Billy Wagner.

One of Randolph's strengths as manager is that he never throws a Pity Party. Some may consider that cold, but the reality is Randolph knows there is no time to languish in a world of self-pity when bad things happen.

"It's no big deal," Randolph said of Sanchez' loss. "Things happen during a long season. What are you going to do? Go crazy."

Randolph owns a player's mentality and he should be commended for that. Ballplayers only want to deal with what's going on at that moment and so Randolph was going to use all the arms in his bullpen to try to make up for the difficult loss of Sanchez.

***

In the win over the Phils, Tom Glavine managed to produce his first victory since June 23. Glavine told reporters after the game that he had been thinking too much.

Pedro Martinez scowls in the first inning of a game against the Philadelphia Phillies.

Florida Marlins second baseman Alfredo Amezaga is late on tagging out Jose Reyes at second base.

Pitching coach Rick Peterson explained the situation, telling the *New York Times*, "If you took a black box and recorded a pitcher's thoughts during a game and listened to them when he's doing well and when he isn't, there's a huge difference. It's not like Tommy's lost at sea here. Over 100 pitches, the difference between a great start and a good one is, what, two pitches? So that means that you have to be two percent better. That's not much for a pitcher like Tom Glavine."

No, it's not.

Glavine got his win and Billy Wagner earned a shaky save only because Wright made a tremendous play on Mike Lieberthal's smash with runners on the corners and two outs. Winning teams find a way.

***

The Mets' past and present collided for three games at Shea the second week of the month. Their 4-3 win over the Padres on Aug. 9 showed that this was a new era. Ex-Met Mike Piazza clubbed two home runs and nearly had a third, but the Mets held on for a win and their fourth straight victory.

They were back on track and owned a 13-game lead over the second-place Phillies.

After the first home run Mets fans gave Piazza a curtain call, something that is rarely done for an opposing player. The second home run the fans weren't quite as nice to Piazza. They had offered their long goodbye. It was time to move on now. In the eighth, when his bid for a third home run fell short, they cheered the out. The 2006 Mets were the most important players at Shea.

Both of the home runs came against Pedro Martinez, who was still trying to get his act together. Piazza said the curtain call was something he will remember for the rest of his life and was truly touched by the fans' show of love.

"I hoped they would settle down, but they didn't," Piazza told reporters. "Being on the home field, the last thing I want to do is show up the other team, but the bottom line is that this game is nothing without the fans. So when they ask you to go, you go and hope (the Mets) understand. I have so much history with those fans."

Everyone understood. This used to be Piazza's town, Piazza's ballpark. And in many ways this was

Orlando Hernandez winds up for a pitch in the Mets' 7-3 victory over the San Diego Padres. Hernandez improved his record to 8-8 with the win.

Jose Valentin tags out San Diego Padres' Dave Roberts who tried to stretch a third-inning single into a double.

Jose Reyes dives safety into second base against the Marlins.

the perfect sendoff for the greatest hitting catcher of all time. It was the best of both worlds for Mets fans. They got to say goodbye to their hero in a great way. Piazza was always about hitting the big home run and they still got to cheer the home team as the victory march toward October continued.

Noted Mets catcher, Paul Lo Duca, "I don't think I've ever seen a curtain call on the road. Pretty cool."

Pretty cool, indeed. It usually never ends that well in New York, but Piazza was a special Met and he will be remembered that way forever. And now these new Mets could get on with their job of trying to bring back post-season glory to Shea Stadium.

This was a critical month for Billy Wagner. The closer made a key adjustment that made a huge difference. Wagner admitted that he had been getting Inner-Half Happy, meaning he was trying to throw his fastball only over the inside of the plate. That allowed hitters to look in and not worry about the outer half of the plate.

Essentially, they only had to cover half the plate.

Realizing this, Wagner made an effort to use his blazing fastball on the outer half and that helped him put together six straight saves by the middle of August. He blew away the Nationals, 3-1, on August 13 for his 28th save. Using the entire plate and throwing 98, the lefty was dominating again.

John Maine unleashes heat during a game against the Washington Nationals.

Pedro Martinez has a friendly conversation with first-base umpire Eric Cooper.

In that game, the Mets also got a huge lift from Michael Tucker, who was called up from Norfolk after Cliff Floyd was lost again to Achilles problems. For Floyd it was one setback after another all season. Tucker hit the go-ahead home run, his first major league home run since July 17, 2005. The Nationals had released Tucker so this was payback. His addition was another one of the quiet Minaya moves that proved so successful.

***

The Mets had put themselves in a position to regroup for the post-season while other NL contenders had to battle to survive. The Cardinals were struggling mightily, having just snapped an eight-game losing streak and were in a battle with the Reds for the Central crown.

Out in the West, Piazza's Padres were fighting the Dodgers for the lead. Not only had the Mets locked up the NL East, but also they were virtually assured of having the best record in baseball and that means they were on tap to play the NL wild card winner,

Billy Wagner celebrates after the Mets won a game 6-5 against the Florida Marlins.

Paul Lo Duca tries to put the tag on the Philadelphia Phillies' Jimmy Rollins. In the background Ryan Howard signals Rollins safe.

unless the wild card came from the East.

In baseball, though, nothing is promised. The calf injury to Pedro Martinez on Aug. 14 was proof of that. Martinez allowed six runs in the first inning of a 13-0 loss to the Phillies. The calf strain was in Martinez' right leg. He also had problems with his right hip and his chronic right toe. Perhaps they were all related because of the torque Martinez puts on his right side when he pitches.

Explained pitching coach Rick Peterson, "The dif-ference between Pedro's torque and another pitcher's torque is the difference between a lot of wind and a tornado."

Martinez wanted this to be the Mets' year in so many ways because when he left the Red Sox as a free agent, the Mets had promised him, as he noted, they would bring in the players needed to "build a championship team around me and Tommy Glavine."

Would the Mets be able to weather this storm? A huge challenge was still in front of them, but they were ready for it just as they were ready for every other challenge they faced in the 2006 season.

To a man, they felt, this was their time, their season of magic. ●

Michael Tucker celebrates his home run with Jose Reyes in a game against the Washington Nationals.

Bye-Bye Boos

Beltran & Lo Duca Prove They Can Make It Anywhere

There is a gauntlet all new players run in New York. It doesn't matter what you did in your old city. No one really cares. What are you going to do here?

This is the big time. This is the place where you make your name or have your spirit broken.

What a difference a year makes. After Carlos Beltran signed a seven-year, $119 million contract, the free agent centerfielder was buried by the boo birds at Shea Stadium in 2005. He couldn't get them off his back. In 2006 he turned those boos into cheers.

When Beltran first arrived, Mets fans were spoiled. They wanted the same production from the slugging switch hitter that the Astros got from Beltran in the 2004 post-season.

No player was as hot as Beltran was that October. Beltran tied a post-season record with eight home runs. He hit .455 in the Astros Division Series five-game victory over the Braves with four home runs, nine RBI and 10 hits. He even stole two bases in that series.

Then in the NLCS against the Cardinals, Beltran nearly single-handedly beat St. Louis. In those seven games Beltran batted .417 with four more home runs and 10 more hits. It wasn't enough. Even though he had 10 hits and four home runs, Beltran only had five RBI. He couldn't do it alone.

The whirlwind off-season followed and the negotiations with Beltran's agent Scott Boras resulted in Beltran landing safely at Shea. The fans wanted the same kind of production from the five-tool player. Instead, Beltran managed only a .266 average. When you're getting paid $119 million to star in New York, that doesn't cut it. Just ask A-Rod.

Instead of bashing eight home runs in 12 post-season games, Beltran managed only 16 home runs in 151 games. In 2005, Beltran did not let the game come to him, he tried to force the issue and when you are a hitter, if you try too hard, you get in trouble. He was jumping at the pitches. He wasn't smooth at the plate.

"You can just see Carlos squeezing the bat," manager Willie Randolph said during Beltran's struggles. "He has to relax a little bit."

It took a year, but Beltran finally learned to relax as a Met. Of course, you can be a lot more relaxed when Carlos Delgado becomes your teammate and in 2006 Beltran had the luxury of hitting in front of Delgado. That's similar to hitting in front of David Ortiz. Good things happen.

Opposing pitchers throw more fastballs to you and Beltran knew what to do with them: hit them hard, hit them in the gaps or hit them over the fence. Going into the third week in August, he had clubbed 33 home runs, fifth best in the NL.

In one season Beltran went from Most Disappointing Player to being a candidate for Most Valuable Player. He learned to deal with New York. He had a blast at the All-Star Game in Pittsburgh. He

Carlos Beltran and Xavier Nady celebrate after defeating the Atlanta Braves 10-6 in Atlanta. Beltran hit two home runs in the game to help the Mets sweep the Braves.

made the most of his opportunities. He was healthy.

Randolph's faith in Beltran never wavered. Randolph has been around too many stars to know that if you can produce in the post-season like Beltran produced in 2004, you don't lose that talent overnight. Beltran was too good a player to struggle like that again.

On the first day of spring training in 2006 Randolph said, "I'm looking forward to Carlos being a big-time player for us. He's going to have a big year. Our core guys have a nice character to them. I feel good that they are strong enough to deal with a lot of stuff that we are going to have to deal with."

Once again Randolph had hit the nail on the head. His baseball vision is usually 20-20. He knew Beltran was poised for a monster year.

Five months later, Randolph had to chuckle when he gave a day off to Beltran. Randolph believes in resting his regulars, it gives them strength down the stretch. He knew the Mets season was not going to end on Oct. 1 like it would end for 11 other teams in the National League. He knew he had to think big picture and he had the lead to give such a break to his core players.

So after a week that included upper 90s temperatures, Randolph decided to give Beltran a rest in a day game against the Padres following a night game.

"I'll rest him here and there, I like to do that," Randolph said. "He's okay. He has aches and pains like everybody else. Nothing serious...if he's going to be the MVP, a day or two (off) isn't going to affect it."

Yes, what a difference a year makes.

"This game is all about statistics," Beltran told Bryan Hoch of *Inside Pitch* magazine. "This game is about being able to go out there and produce and help the team win. Coming to New York, people expect a lot from players, including myself. But the reality was that I wasn't feeling good, and I did the best I could, you know?

"If you have an opportunity where there's a ball in the gap, you have a chance to get it," Beltran said. "When you're not [healthy], you're not going to have a chance. You can't get to first or make those plays when you're hurt, because you're going to be thinking about the injury. This year, I'm not hurt or thinking about anything. I'm just thinking about going out there and giving everything I can. If I have a good day, good. But if I don't, I still feel like I'm healthy."

Early in the year he noted that location has nothing to do with success.

"When you have the ability and the talent to do it, it doesn't matter where you play," said Beltran, who had played in small markets Kansas City and Houston. "If you stay healthy, you'll be fine. And I'll be fine."

Beltran couldn't stay healthy in 2005 and it all started with a strained right quad that slowed him for weeks. It kept him out 10 days but bothered him much longer than that. Beltran probably should have gone on the disabled list.

Then when Beltran finally was feeling good he was involved in a frightening collision with Mike Cameron in San Diego on August 11. Beltran suffered a minimally displaced facial fracture and a concussion on the play that saw Cameron suffer serious multiple facial fractures.

In his own way, Beltran showed Mets fans just how tough he was by hanging in there for what was the most difficult season of his career. Despite all the problems, Beltran still managed to drive in 78 runs. From the left side he hit .308 and in September he put together a 10-game hitting streak.

"It was tough," Beltran admitted in spring training. "It took me like two months to be 100 percent, and when I was feeling better at the plate I had the collision with Mike. Last year, to me it's in the past. This year I'm looking forward to a new season; to show the fans and everyone what I'm capable of doing. I know if I stayed healthy the entire year, I

Carlos Beltran follows through on a two-run home run off Florida Marlins starting pitcher Scott Olsen.

Paul Lo Duca blocks the plate as Josh Wellingham of the Florida Marlins slides into home.

would have done a better job."

Beltran wanted to do everything in his power to put the 2005 season behind him. Hard work got him to this point in his career, so he made an effort to work harder in the off-season.

Beltran had a batting cage built in his house in Manati, Puerto Rico and hit every day. He even used the cage on Christmas Day. "Every day," he said with a smile. "Every year you have to prove yourself. Because if you have a good year, people say, 'Well, it's just one year.' If you have another good year, 'Well, maybe this year won't be so good.' So you have to prove yourself every year and I feel like that."

That's exactly the kind of player Omar Minaya wanted when he signed Beltran. At the age of 29, Beltran is just beginning to reach his prime.

The best thing about the 2006 Mets is that to a man they felt they were the best team in the NL East from the first day of the year. They were confident. Beltran exhibited that confidence when he told reporters before the season, "I just believe this has to be our year. If we stay healthy and we find a way to play the game right, I don't see why we can't win the division."

He was right. There were difficult times early in the year with the fans. Every time Beltran made an out, fans booed him.

That booing prompted teammates and Minaya to stand up for their centerfielder. "The fans here,

Paul Lo Duca looks to the dugout for a call from his manager during a game against the Cincinnati Reds.

they're demanding and they're tough, but not always fair," Minaya said at the time. He knew it takes a tough-minded individual to play in New York.

Beltran didn't waver. He had confidence in his ability. During one game when he turned the boos to cheers, Beltran had to be coaxed out of the dugout by veteran Julio Franco.

"If I stay healthy, I know I'm capable to do a lot of good things on the baseball field," Beltran said. "And I know I can help the team win ballgames."

And he did throughout the summer, including when the Mets delivered an 11-run inning against the Cubs at Wrigley Field in July and Beltran bashed a grand slam in the second in the inning. Cliff Floyd hit the first grand slam of the inning.

That day in Chicago, Beltran was so excited about what the Mets were doing in the incredible inning, he told reporters that he didn't realize the bases were loaded when he hit his home run. "I never saw the guy on third," he said. "But then I saw three guys at home plate, so I was excited."

That also was a sign that Beltran was relaxed at the plate, the same kind of approach he had with the Astros in 2004 during October, getting big hits when it mattered most.

While the addition of his close friend Delgado helped Beltran immensely and closer Billy Wagner strengthened the bullpen, there was one other key addition made by Minaya in the off-season that put the pieces of the puzzle together for the Mets. That was the trade for catcher Paul Lo Duca, another tough-minded player.

Off the field, Lo Duca was going through a messy divorce, on the field he was a no-nonsense leader for the Mets, who played hurt and guided the pitching staff. Lo Duca was named to the All-Star team in July, the fourth straight season he was named an All-Star. Going into the season, Lo Duca's 659 hits over the last five years was the third most by a catcher over that span.

After pulling off the trade for Lo Duca, Minaya said, "When the off-season began, we had three main priorities: to fortify our bullpen, add an impact middle-of-the-lineup presence and solidify our catching. We feel we have addressed those needs with Billy Wagner, Carlos Delgado and now Paul Lo Duca."

Minaya knows the value of veterans. Lo Duca was pivotal behind the plate and also batting second in the lineup. Randolph needed someone in that spot who could handle the bat and help push Jose Reyes around the bases, thus setting up Beltran and Delgado. Offensively, Lo Duca did much better than the Mets expected as he and David Wright were the only two starters batting over .300 heading into the middle of August.

The Mets saw what kind of player they were getting in Lo Duca in the season opener, when he dropped the ball on a tag at home of Alfonso Soriano on a key play, but he still sold the call to the umpire. Even though Soriano was clearly safe, Lo Duca's acting job did the trick.

Joked Lo Duca later, "I'm a magician in the off-season."

Replacing an icon like Mike Piazza is no easy task. Lo Duca's grittiness helped him do the job. Lo Duca managed to keep the revolving door pitching staff together. He kept them on task. Lo Duca downplayed his guidance of that staff to MLB.com, saying, "Most of the guys we've had come through here this season have pitched in the big leagues. They're polished. They don't need a lot of coaching. Some guys need a pat on the back. Some guys you have to get after. They're all different. You learn their personalities and work with them."

Lo Duca also played through a hand injury during the year, but that's the way he has always played the game. Lo Duca averaged 143 games a season over the previous four years with the Dodgers and Marlins. He straps on the gear and does his job. ●

Paul Lo Duca gets thrown out of the game after arguing with home-plate umpire Angel Hernandez in the first inning of a game against the Atlanta Braves.

True Believer

For Jose Reyes, Being Good Is All In A Day's Work

The young man was fast, but he needed to get faster. There was no money for special training or equipment, so the young man did what had to be done. When you have a dream to play in the major leagues, the desire and the talent, you are already halfway up the mountain of success.

Now, you just have to figure out a way.

So the young man tied a rope around his waist. The rope was connected to an old tire filled with cement. He would drag that tire up the hill, working his muscles to exhaustion. It made him sweat. It made him faster.

"Man, that was hard," Jose Reyes said of his unique workout regimen when he was a teenager. "But that's the way we do it back home. We work with what we have."

Home is the Dominican Republic. His father, Jose, is a baseball coach there. The father recognized early that the son had a gift. He watched him run, an effortless glide. He watched him field, making nearly every play at shortstop, he watched him throw lasers to first base. He watched him smile.

The great ones play the game with a love that cannot be taught. Every day on the baseball field is a joy, win or lose. You either have it or you don't. Jose Reyes Sr. knew that his son had the gift in so many different ways.

"I knew he was going to be a good one when he was about 12 years old," Jose Sr. explained. "He was good and he enjoyed playing baseball. He always loved the game and it showed. He always worked hard to make himself a better ballplayer."

The father is quick to laugh and share his baseball knowledge with his son. "They love my dad back home," Reyes said with his trademark smile. "He knows a lot. He still tells me now I can't swing at the two-strike pitch in the dirt. I'm learning."

He also told his son that he had to work to get better.

That's why Reyes would pull that tire filled with cement up the hill over and over again. You don't have to belong to a fancy gym to get the benefits of training. You just have to believe in yourself.

Jose Reyes believed.

And when the scouts saw him, they believed, too.

The Mets signed Reyes as a non-drafted free agent on August 16, 1999. From that day on the shortstop was considered a can't-miss prospect. It's one thing when scouts notice talent, it's another when ushers do.

Early in spring training of 2003, I was in Port St. Lucie to do a story on Reyes. That previous summer, Reyes played in 42 games for the St. Lucie Mets. I went to Tradition Field, spring training home of the Mets, and home of the Class A Mets. I talked to some of the ushers about their favorite young Met. "Keep an eye on Reyes," they said. "He's special."

One usher put it best: "When Reyes hits a ball in the gap, everybody in the ballpark stops and watches him run. No one goes from first to third like he does."

Tommy Bowes has been head groundskeeper at Tradition Field complex since 1988. He has seen a lot of players come and go. "When Jose's teammates were

Jose Reyes yells to fans. The speedy All-Star shortstop signed a $23.25 million, four-year contract extension with the Mets just before the game.

in the clubhouse, done for the day, he'd still be out on the back field taking ground balls. His work ethic was amazing. And he never lost that smile."

Reyes hit 11 triples in only 69 games at St. Lucie. He was promoted to AA Binghamton, where he lashed eight more triples in 65 games. In 2003 he started the season at AAA Norfolk, was leading the International League with 26 stolen bases in 42 games and was called up to the Mets on June 10, one day before his 20th birthday. He singled his first at-bat. That day he also doubled and scored two runs. He became only the ninth teenager to ever play for the Mets.

All that work, all that energy used pulling that cement-filled tire up the hill had paid off. "This is a dream come true," Reyes said at the time. "This is what I always wanted."

The transaction also marked the last move in the Steve Phillips era. The general manager was fired two days later.

"Bringing a kid like Reyes to the majors is something special," Phillips said in Pittsburgh in July of 2006, a day before Reyes would have been the All-Star starting shortstop for the National League at PNC Park, if not for a hand injury he suffered just before the break. "We always felt that he would be a star."

A few days after being called up, Reyes hit his first major league home run, a grand slam. The kid had a flair for the dramatic, becoming only the second Mets player in history to have his first major-league home run be a grand slam. Jack Hamilton did it on May 20, 1967. Reyes became the youngest player in the majors to blast a grand slam since 1964, when 19-year-old Tony Conigliaro hit one for the Red Sox. The switch-hitting Reyes batted .307 in 69 games with the Mets.

Even a can't-miss prospect can stumble, though, and Reyes was hit with a series of leg injuries, spraining his left ankle on Aug. 31 against the Phillies. The next spring he suffered a strained right hamstring that hobbled him all season. In August he suffered a stress fracture of the left fibula.

"Those were tough times," Reyes said. "But I kept working."

The Mets tried to teach him a new way to run but that was like trying to teach a deer a different way to dash through the woods. Eventually his body healed and Reyes was back on the fast track to being a star.

"I run hard out of the box every time," he said of his style. "You never know what might happen. You have to put the pressure on the other team. That's what I try to do all the time."

That's what excites his teammates every time he steps into the batter's box or takes his position at shortstop. That's what excites the fans and that's why Reyes was voted onto the All-Star team as a starter in 2006, one of the highlights of his short career.

"Being an All-Star is unbelievable," Reyes said. "I watched the game all the time and my favorite players were Robby Alomar and Derek Jeter."

Jeter didn't become an All-Star until 1998 when he was all of 24. Reyes just turned 23, so their paths to stardom are similar.

"The kid is amazing," pitcher Tom Glavine said. "He's exciting, he's fun. He gets better all the time. He's one of those guys that has that rare distinction when you try to project how good he is going to be. You know what? He's going to be as good as he wants to be. If he stays healthy, there's no telling what he can do. It's just remarkable how much better his overall game has gotten since he's arrived."

Jeter isn't thrilled that Reyes considered him a boyhood hero. That means the Yankee captain is getting old, but he does appreciate what Reyes has accomplished. At the All-Star Game he said of Reyes' rise to stardom: "It's good for New York. He's having a great year. I think it's great for Mets fans."

Billy Wagner has been in the majors since 1995 and is amazed by Reyes' talent. "I've never been with a player that can bring so much to the table," Wagner said. "The scary part is he's only 23."

In Willie Randolph, Reyes has the perfect manager.

Jose Reyes dives for a ball hit by the Baltimore Orioles' Brandon Fahey during a recent game.

Like Reyes, Randolph was an All-Star middle infielder at a young age. Reyes is becoming a student of the game under Randolph's tutelage. Randolph says Reyes will become a much better player in the future. On defense he will learn to anticipate the play, he will focus better on every pitch. He will learn the hitters. He will learn to anticipate the play much better than he does now.

"At shortstop, you have a great view of the field," Randolph noted.

At shortstop, if you stay totally focused on each pitch, you will see things before they happen. You will see the hitter's approach, the angle of the bat, the ball out of the pitcher's hand. The great ones see the future.

Reyes is learning all that now, just as David Wright is learning the nuances of third base. That left side of the Mets infield is in sure hands for a decade.

Three hours before a game against the Reds in June, Reyes sits at a table in the center of the Mets clubhouse. He is studying video of Reds starter Bronson Arroyo. When Arroyo drops down to throw one of his Frisbee sliders, Reyes lets out, an "Oh man."

Reyes' exuberance for the game is one of his most endearing traits.

On offense Reyes has taken "baby steps" to improve, Randolph noted.

Those baby steps were good enough to lead the National League in three vital categories: runs, stolen bases and triples, heading down the stretch. Speed is a wonderful thing.

"I think he is going to be a perennial All-Star as we go along," Randolph said of his star. Randolph became an All-Star when he was only 22. He knows what that means to a career. "It's just a matter of him getting that first nod and now Jose has gotten that. I know how great that is to be an All-Star at such a young age and it just sets a tone, and springboards you into that level of upper echelon players where you expect it every year. And it's great for your confidence to rub elbows with those players. That's a good thing to expect from yourself every year," Randolph said.

Reyes loves being in New York. He loves the excitement of the ballpark, and lives just eight minutes from Shea Stadium.

If you see him relaxing at home in his condo, you begin to understand why Reyes is so grounded. His mother Rosa cooks all his meals. He rarely goes out to dinner.

"Why go out when I have the best food here," explained Reyes, who, when he first came to the Mets, could not speak English, but has taught himself the language. "Oh my goodness, is my mom a great cook," Reyes said.

As for learning the language he said he just took the time to do it. "Just talking with my friends, you know, David Wright, people like that, they help me a lot," Reyes explained. "When you're not afraid to speak a language, you're going to learn a lot. If you're going to stay quiet, you're not going to learn."

Reyes is not afraid to learn on or off the field. There is a comfort level to his style of play that many veteran players don't have and he said one of the reasons he is so relaxed is because his family lives in New York with him during the season.

"It's so nice having them here, I don't have to worry about anything," Reyes said. "I got everything I need here."

The heavenly smell of a fine-cooked meal and the feeling of love runs throughout the home that Reyes shares with his girlfriend, their 19-month-old daughter and his mom and dad. Adorable little Katerine, who is named after her mother, scoots around the living room, showing off the same light-up-the-ballpark smile as her dad, the same smile that belongs to Rosa.

Perhaps the best thing about Reyes, besides his incredible talent and love of the game, is that he knows what's important in his life. Leave the late-night partying to others, Reyes has a winning routine he follows during the season.

Jose Reyes watches his eighth-inning home run off Philadelphia Phillies pitcher Ryan Franklin sail into the stands.

Jose Reyes hits a grand slam against the Philadelphia Phillies.

He sleeps in, much like Jeter. He plays with Katerine. "She loves to pull my hair, watch cartoons and dance, being a dad is great," Reyes said proudly. "When I come home from the game she is here waiting for me. She's like me, she stays up late and sleeps late."

Reyes' favorite meals usually include chicken, with side dishes of yucca or plantains. "I'm a chicken guy," he noted. *SportsCenter* is on throughout the morning. For a night game, he heads to the ballpark around 2:15, driving over in his Hummer H2 with the sparkling 25-inch rims, a vehicle he purchased from ex-Met Mike Cameron.

Reyes favorite play is the triple. Of course. "Every time I hit a ball into the gap, I'm going to hustle all the way to third base, 99 percent I'm going to go to third," he said of his mindset out of the batter's box.

You can tell Reyes is an entertainer by the way he plays shortstop, but he also loves to sing. Reggaeton is his favorite music and once in a while he performs on the team bus, a regular Don Omar or Daddy Yankee. He loves to sing in front of his friends back at home in Santiago in the Dominican.

"That's my hobby in the Dominican, when I get some friends at the house," he explained. "I have a microphone and everything."

Reyes played on the Dominican team in the World Baseball Classic in the spring of 2006. Even though he didn't start, he considered it an honor to be on the team, to be around his heroes and he used that time to entertain them. Reyes was the life of the party, singing on the bus and in the clubhouse.

When Reyes comes home from Shea, the first thing he does is turn on the TV to an out-of-town game as Rosa cooks another delicious plate of food. Reyes is an observant person. "I was always that way," he said. He knows how the 25th man on the Mariners is performing because he watches so many games.

"Jose is incredible," explained Chris Leible, one of his agents and a close friend. "He knows about every player on every team. What they're hitting, how they're playing. He's a baseball encyclopedia."

Reyes smiled at those words and said, "I love the game and I enjoy life. It's great, man."

He's climbed that hill. ●

Jose Reyes slaps a double in the ninth inning against the St. Louis Cardinals.

Future Perfect

The Best Is Yet To Come For Both Mets' Players And Fans

The future has never been brighter for the Mets. There is a wealth of young talent in the organization, some already at the major league level, and a new ballpark is set to be built in time for the 2009 season. From all reports, this is not just any new park but one that promises to be magnificent in every way.

After living with dingy Shea Stadium for so long, Mets fans deserve such a ballpark, a ballpark that is clean and luxurious and has all the amenities of other new ballparks--a ballpark as exciting as New York.

"It's going to be perfect," said Dave Howard, the Mets' executive vice president of business operations.

The plans seem perfect and on the day that Mets chairman and CEO Fred Wilpon unveiled those golden plans, he thought back to his childhood and how special it was to go to Ebbets Field. "I almost feel like I'm walking through the rotunda, eight or nine years old, holding my dad's hand," the Brooklyn native said at the press conference, becoming emotional at the memory.

Most fans could relate to Wilpon's words because baseball has forever been a game of fathers and sons, a game they share in such a special way. That is the beauty of baseball.

Fred Wilpon has always felt close to the Brooklyn Dodgers and as a result has always wanted to have a new ballpark for his team and fans, the kind of park that was truly special, a baseball home, not a multi-purpose stadium like Shea, which is antiquated in nearly every way.

The Wilpons want the new ballpark to be a place where a grandfather can take his grandson, where fathers and mothers can take sons and daughters, a place of family. They want it to be a place where different baseball generations can come together to watch the game and enjoy each other's company.

The seats beyond first and third base will be articulated toward second base, meaning fans will not have to crane their necks to watch the action. That seems like such a simple concept but yet in so many ballparks, even some new ones, the seats aren't turned toward the action of the infield.

That common sense approach promises to make the Mets' new park a New York landmark. "We're going to have wide seats with extra legroom, wide aisles, wide concourses," Howard said, excited at the prospect of all the newness after years of being saddled with Shea. "I can't compare anything that will be done at the new park to Shea because Shea does not have any of these features that we plan to do."

Essentially, this new park will be a new world for Mets fans. They are finally stepping into a new baseball century.

"We have a tremendous opportunity here to make this right," Howard said.

Roger Craig in action against the Milwaukee Braves at the Polo Grounds in New York City, May 12, 1962.

The suites will be right, simply because they will be located in fair territory, something Shea doesn't really offer. There will be lots of seating in the outfield, too, something that is not a reality at Shea.

"We have benches, but not many outfield seats in fair territory," said Jeff Wilpon, the club's senior vice president and chief operating officer. "Seats in fair territory are a must at the new park. We learned a lot from the building of the park in Brooklyn. We want this to be a place where multi-generations of fans can enjoy themselves in different ways, where people can mill about on the concourse and you can still see the game."

So when you're buying that hot dog you won't miss any of the action.

Jeff Wilpon said there will be good seats at all price ranges so the average fan is not priced out of the new park. That is a must. The Mets don't want this to be some corporate ballpark, where fans go only to cut a business deal. They want passionate fans at the games. They want it to be a park that all their fans can enjoy so the Mets still have that feel that they are the people's team, much like the Brooklyn Dodgers.

The new park will be built next to Shea Stadium. It will seat around 42,000 fans to keep it intimate and there will be about 3,000 standing room tickets available. The Mets do not want capacity to go over 45,000 because they want it to feel like a ballpark, not a stadium.

There will be a rotunda as you enter behind home plate, evoking the spirit of Ebbets Field, but the other parts of the park will be unique in their design. The Yankees also will be opening the new Yankee Stadium in 2009, so New York, after being left behind by so many other cities where new stadiums have been built, will be back at the forefront of ballparks.

The new Mets park will also have a state of the art press box, something that has been lacking in some of the other new parks. Since New York is the media capitol of the world, that only seems fitting.

There will be 58 luxury suites in the new Mets park and all the suites will have interior and exterior seating. Shea only has interior seating for their so-called suites.

There also will be a new restaurant where you can actually watch all the action from every table. The current restaurant at Shea has an extremely limited view of the field and that view is only provided for a small number of tables near the front. You basically have to put your face in your plate to see a small portion of the field.

The new park will also have many more bathrooms than Shea, another plus.

In fairness to Shea, this is a ballpark from a much different era. It should have been torn down a long time ago. It did not age well like Dodger Stadium.

Shea opened on April 17, 1964 when the Pirates beat the Mets, 4-3, behind the pitching of Bob Friend. Shea is widely considered the most difficult park to play in for a number of reasons. There is the chilling cold in the early season, the wind, the airplanes above, and the tricky infield that has eaten up many an infielder, including Kaz Matsui.

After coming to the Mets as a free agent, Cliff Floyd once asked, "Does it ever get warm here?" Considering Floyd is from Chicago and owns a home in Toronto, that is quite a statement.

First baseman Tim Harkness holds the distinction of making the first out as a Met in Shea, when he grounded out in that 1964 opener. He also holds the distinction of being the first Met to get a hit at Shea when he laced a third-inning single off Friend.

There were other significant Shea firsts, including Al Jackson throwing the first shutout there on April 19, 1964, when he blanked the Pirates, 6-0 on a six hitter. Hall of Famer Bill Mazeroski, perhaps the greatest fielding second baseman of all time, holds the distinction of making the first error at Shea on April 17, 1964, a sign of trouble for the difficult infield.

The 1964 All-Star Game was played at brand new Shea Stadium and the National League won its seventh straight game on July 7, beating the American League, 7-4. The All-Star Game never came back to Shea.

Willie Mays started the winning rally in the ninth with a walk and a stolen base. Mays started in center-

Tommie Agee connects for a first-inning home run off of Baltimore Orioles pitcher Jim Palmer in a World Series game at Shea Stadium in New York, Oct. 14, 1969.

field and played the entire game. He came around to score on an infield single by Orlando Cepeda coupled with an error from the Yankees Joe Pepitone. Second baseman Ron Hunt became the first Met to start an All-Star Game that day.

Shea had other great moments. It saw the glory of the 1969 Miracle Mets, of Hank Aaron hitting a home run in Game 3, the only game at Shea of the series and the third homer of the series for Aaron as the Mets swept away Atlanta. A young pitcher came on in relief that day and pitched seven shutout innings for the Mets.

This was a sign of things to come, but that performance wasn't enough to keep the Mets from later trading away Nolan Ryan. And this generation of Mets fans thinks the Scott Kazmir trade was bad.

Those Mets, who had been lovable losers up until this point in their history, went on to win the World Series against the heavily favored Orioles in five games. The last three games of the Series were played at Shea with the Mets winning all three.

The pitching was spectacular. Gary Gentry and Ryan, who got the save by pitching 2 1/3 innings of relief, combined to shut out the Orioles 5-0 in Game Three as a raucous crowd of 56,335 went bonkers. Tommie Agee hit a leadoff home run off Jim Palmer and the Mets never looked back. Amazingly, that was the only leadoff home run that Palmer would ever allow in his Hall of Fame career, but that's what made those Mets so Amazin'. Agee also made a great sprawling catch in the seventh.

In Game Four Tom Seaver was not to be denied. He went all 10 innings to beat the Orioles, 2-1. That was the game where Ron Swoboda made his full-length, diving catch. Everything the Mets did that year turned to gold. In the 10th J.C. Martin pinch-hit for Seaver. Martin put down a bunt with Rod Gaspar at second, and sometimes the littlest things are the most important. Pitcher Pete Richert's throw hit Martin, the ball went into right field and Gaspar scored to put the Mets one win away from their first championship.

Then came fateful Game Five. The Orioles led 3-0 but the Mets came back on the strength of home runs by Donn Clendenon and Al Weis. Swoboda's RBI double gave the Mets the lead in the eighth. The final out came when Jerry Koosman got Davey Johnson to fly out to Cleon Jones in left. New York partied.

Johnson, of course, would be the manager of the wild bunch, the 1986 Mets that pulled off their own World Series shocker, beating the Red Sox in a classic World Series. To get there the Mets had to win the classic Game Six of the League Championship Series at the AstroDome. This was a heavyweight fight, both sides trading knockout punches, but in the end, the three runs the Mets scored in the top of the 16th held up as the Astros came back to score two in the bottom of the inning. Jesse Orosco struck out Kevin Bass to become the first pitcher to collect three wins in one LCS.

By the time the Red Sox came to town the Mets were drained and it showed as they lost the first two games at Shea, falling 1-0 and 9-3. The Mets bats were dead, but Lenny Dykstra led off Game Three at Fenway with a home run and the Mets had their mojo going strong again. They won Games Three and Four to tie the Series but the Red Sox took Game Five and now had a 3-2 lead as the two teams came back to Shea. On the night of Oct. 25 the Mets went into the bottom of the 10th inning trailing, 5-3. They somehow found a way to win and baseball lore was written. Mookie Wilson hit a little dribbler up the first base line. The ball went through Bill Buckner's legs and the rest is history.

Ray Knight came bounding home with the winning run as 55,078 Mets fans were sure they had witnessed a miracle. Red Sox Nation thought it was forever cursed.

A day of rain followed, and then Knight again helped to win Game Seven, blasting a seventh-inning home run that gave the Mets the lead for good.

It's been 20 years since the Mets last won a World Series. For most of that time Mets fans have been living in the past, reliving the wild and crazy moments from the 1969 and 1986 World Series.

A generation of Mets fans has come and gone, won-

The Mets' Miracle 2006 Season

Catcher Gary Carter leaps on his teammates as they celebrate their 6-5 victory over the Boston Red Sox in the 10th inning of Game Six of the World Series at Shea Stadium, Saturday, Oct. 25, 1986. Boston was one out away from winning the championship before the Mets rallied for three runs and a victory. The Mets went on to win the World Series in Game 7.

dering when will the team win another World Series?

It's back to the future now and these new Mets are hoping to make their own history.

No matter what happens, whether or not Shea ever again sees another World Championship, the Mets appear to be a franchise in good hands for quite some time. They have the look and feel of winners.

The goal is to get to the post-season and see what happens. As the Mets proved in '69 and '86 anything is possible. Dreams come true. Legends are created. Baseball history is made when no one expects it.

The goal for these Mets is to be consistent every season. Not just show up every once in a while, but to be a playoff team every year. In the mediocre National League that can be accomplished. The Mets have the money and the desire to build championship teams, and they are in it for the long haul with Minaya leading the way.

Some of their top prospects will be with the club by 2009 and be new stars, making the new park home to a championship caliber team.

The Mets already have the nucleus of that team set. Barring injury, Jose Reyes is locked in at short as is David Wright at third. They are the cornerstone players of the club and have both signed contract extensions. Carlos Beltran should be around as well in centerfield. If Lastings Milledge is not traded, he also will be a key player.

Minaya wants to make the new Mets an athletic club. The ballpark's dimensions will be much like the current Shea dimensions spiced up by a series of nooks and crannies, so it is imperative that the Mets have athletes.

The Mets do not want the new park to be a pitcher's nightmare like some of the current new parks. They want the park to play fair and not wear out their pitching staff.

That staff figures to be anchored in 2009 by Mike Pelfry, the Mets first-round pick in 2005. The Mets also are high on Brian Bannister, who made a great impression with the club this season before suffering a hamstring injury.

Perhaps the most intriguing player that the Mets are hopeful of becoming a star come 2009 is 20-year-old outfielder Carlos Gomez, who was the youngest player in the Eastern League in 2006.

Scouts are raving over Gomez. Said one longtime scout, "I'm not saying he's Willie Mays, but Carlos Gomez plays the game with the same kind of energy that Mays did. He's going to be something special."

If you are a centerfielder and your name is mentioned in any way with the Say Hey Kid, you're doing something extremely right.

Gomez glides effortlessly in centerfield. His route to fly balls still needs polish, but the diamond is beginning to shine. He can throw from the right-center gap to third on a line and he can hit with power and run.

Gomez has a great frame, at 6-4, 195, and he's a Top-Step Player. When his team is at-bat, he watches from the top step, just like Derek Jeter. He's not sitting back talking about where he's going after the game, he's learning on every pitch. That is how a young player gets better.

In many ways, Gomez seems to be the complete package. If he is, the Mets outfield will be set for many years to come. Gomez said he is hopeful of playing in the majors in 2007. He has incredible speed. "He's faster than Jose Reyes," Minaya said. What Gomez has to learn to do is use that speed in baseball fashion as Reyes has done. Reyes is three years older than Gomez, who is also from the Dominican.

Like Reyes, Gomez owns a wonderful smile and lives to play the game. "Jose and I are good friends," Gomez said. "We work out together in the winter."

The Mets also signed the son of Yankee coach Tony Pena, 16-year-old Francisco Pena. Pena cannot play professionally until he turns 17. Minaya has proven he is not afraid to move young talent up the ladder quickly and Pena said that entered into his thinking when he signed with the Mets, telling reporters "I think I have an opportunity to get to the big leagues faster. I am more familiar with the minor league coaches and staff."

Minaya said he loves the fact that Pena comes from a baseball family, and that is a trend he is trying to

Omar Minaya had a bold vision when he was hired in 2004, and has set up the Mets to have a bright future.

develop. The Mets have clearly switched their emphasis to players who are not only good at the game, the talent has to be there, but they are going after players who love the game.

That is the only way to produce winning teams. A player like Reyes has been around the game all his life. His father was a coach in the Dominican and that kind of player respects the game. Those players will work harder in the long run to get to the next level.

Same goes for David Wright. The Mets can only hope that someone like Francisco Pena follows the same plan. You have to find gamers as well as talented players and that's another reason why signing Reyes and Wright to long-term contract extensions was so important.

The message the Mets sent to their young players is that "We want you to be like Reyes and Wright. We want young players who are talented, but who are also good citizens that can be models of success."

Signing too many free agents can destroy a franchise from within. There has to be a combination of home-grown players interspersed with players from the free agent market.

And by signing a player like Pedro Martinez as a free agent that only raises the Mets standing in the Dominican. The Martinez signing will pay huge dividends long after Pedro is done pitching because he is so loved in his home country.

Minaya's staff is good at looking at all the pieces of the puzzle and then putting it together from every perspective, from management's perspective and from the player's perspective.

John Ricco is the Mets assistant GM and he paid his dues by working 12 years in the commissioner's office in a variety of roles. His last job there was the director, contract salary administrator for MLB, essentially managing all non-legal functions of the labor relations department. He's a man who knows contracts and the rules inside and out, has conducted player salary analysis for years so he is an expert in the field.

Tony Bernazard is the special assistant to the GM and before that he was a special assistant with the Major League Baseball Players Association and served the union as a player development liaison, constantly communicating with the players.

Between Bernazard and Ricco, both sides of the street, MLB management and the Players Association, are covered. That is smart business.

Minaya also has surrounded himself with trusted and longtime scouts, his top scout being Sandy Johnson, who is special assistant to the GM. Johnson came from the Diamondbacks where he was vice president and senior assistant general manager. Johnson is deeply respected in the scouting family and in 2005 he won the Roland Hemond award for lifetime achievement by Baseball America.

His resume also includes this impressive note. In 2000, he was a member of the USA Baseball Election Committee, the group that selected the team won the Gold Medal in Sydney. So everywhere he goes, Johnson is trying to win the gold.

Johnson has known Minaya since the mid-80s when Johnson was with the Rangers. Before that he was with the Padres. He is instrumental in signing such players as Benito Santiago, Mitch Williams, Sandy Alomar Jr., Juan Gonzalez, Pudge Rodriguez, Sammy Sosa, Robb Nen and Kevin Brown.

Other top scouts like Bill Livesey, Al Goldis, Bryan Lambe and Gary LaRocque are in the Mets front office. Lambe worked for the Diamondbacks from 200-2005 and helped fill that system with quality young players.a

Scouting is the basis of a team's success. Too many teams nowadays simply scout by computer, leaving out the human element. Numbers have a big place in the game, a place that is growing larger every year, but this is not a fantasy league, numbers can play tricks on you and that's why there has to be a combination of scouting by sight and scouting by numbers.

If that all works out, if the young players progress and the new ballpark is built as advertised, the Mets and their fans will have their own slice of baseball heaven. ●

Since Omar Minaya brought Willie Randolph on board as manager soon after his own hiring, the Mets organization has had a lot to smile about.

Carlos Beltran and David Wright form a nucleus for the Mets that will serve as a strong foundation for years to come.